the ORIGINAL PHILADELPHIA Neighborhood COOKBOOK

by
Irina Smith & Ann Hazan

the ORIGINAL PHILADELPHIA Neighborhood COOKBOOK

by

Irina Smith & *Ann Hazan*

Designed & Illustrated by Amy Blake

CAMINO BOOKS
Philadelphia

Manufactured in the United States of America

1 2 3 4 5 91 90 89 88

Library of Congress Cataloging in Publication Data

Smith, Irina, 1942-
   The original Philadelphia neighborhood cookbook.

   Includes index.
   1. Cookery, American. 2. Cookery—Pennsylvania—
Philadelphia. I. Hazan, Ann 1946- II. Title.

TX715.S6527   1987   641.5   87-16656
ISBN 0-940159-02-3

For information write:

Publisher
Camino Books
P.O. Box 59026
Philadelphia, PA 19102
U.S.A.

Cover recipe: Mediterranean Chicken, p. 105.

To our mothers, by whose sides we learned to cook,
and to our husbands, who stood by our sides
through the testings and tastings.

# Contents

 # Introduction

As we walked through the many sections of Philadelphia, talking with the people and gathering recipes for this book, we came to realize just how fortunate we are to live in a city whose neighborhoods offer such a wide variety of cuisines and cooking styles. To collect the recipes for this book, we traveled miles by car and foot to over 50 Philadelphia neighborhoods tasting and testing the favorite recipes from the people who live and work there. We visited private homes, local shops, places of worship, medical centers, neighborhood restaurants, diners, and taverns to bring you appetizers, entrees, desserts and a variety of ethnic dishes for every season and occasion. We watched the preparation of each recipe and then tested, measured ingredients, and standardized these family favorites for all of us to follow in our own kitchens and enjoy in our homes.

Philadelphia is known today as a city of neighborhoods but when William Penn founded his "greene Countrie Towne" in 1681, the neighborhoods we think of today were nowhere to be found. In their place were the farms of Dutch, English, and Swedish settlers, many of which had been purchased from the local Delaware and Lenni-Lenape tribes.

From the beginning, Philadelphia and independent villages like Germantown, attracted diverse groups. The guarantee of freedom of worship was attractive to many who had fled religious persecution.

One group that can trace its roots in Philadelphia back to the earliest years did not originally come here by choice. The first blacks in this area were slaves brought here by the Dutch 50 years before the arrival of William Penn.

By the early 18th century, Philadelphia had 2,500 inhabitants and had become the gateway through which Europeans in great numbers passed on their way to making new lives for themselves and their descendants. Between 1726 and 1755, 40,000 Germans arrived. They were joined after 1730 by settlers from impoverished Northern Ireland. And our city's first practicing Jew, Nathan Levy, came to stay in 1735.

By 1765, there were approximately 5,000 dwellings in Philadelphia, housing a population of 25,000. By contrast, Boston's population was a more modest 15,000. Philadelphia had become after London, the largest city under the British crown.

Nevertheless, on the eve of the American Revolution, Philadelphia was still a city whose neighborhoods could be covered in an afternoon's walk. This was to change dramatically in the next century. By 1860, the city boasted half a million inhabitants living in an area of nearly 130 square miles.

Despite population changes and shifts, Philadelphia remained a city of immigrants. In 1890, the city was home to 110,000 Irish and 75,000 Germans. And still ahead was a new wave of immigration which by 1910 had seen the arrival of 90,000 Russians and 45,000 Italians. Philadelphia's natural trade routes with the South and its location just above the Mason-Dixon line contributed to the growth of the largest black community in any Northern city.

Almost from the beginning Philadelphia was a major inland port, and in the 19th century it became a busy rail center. These advantages promoted Philadelphia's ethnic diversity, bringing people from countries as far away as China and as disparate as Puerto Rico and Poland.

Walking through the neighborhoods of Philadelphia today, we can appreciate the results of all this: the mixture of languages and dialects, the fascinating food stores, and the wonderful exotic cooking aromas from all over the world—all combining to make Philadelphia a truly international city. And nowhere is this more evident than in the kitchens and simmering pots of its neighborhoods.

Come with us now as we enter those kitchens and lift the lids off those pots.

 # Acknowledgments

We enjoyed collecting, testing and tasting each recipe included in this book. However, our greatest pleasure was in meeting and getting to know the many people who helped make this book possible.

We would like to thank all the wonderful people in the many Philadelphia neighborhoods we visited, who willingly and generously shared with us, and now with you, their most treasured recipes. We hope no one has been omitted inadvertently.

Rama Assar *University City*
Linda Baker *Center City*
Joanie Barba *Queen Village*
Della Barbour *Fishtown*
Angela Rodriguez Batt *The Parkway*
Glen Bennington *Roxborough*
Eleanor Bilunas *Port Richmond*
Mariette Bitar *Bella Vista*
Diane Blassingale *South Philadelphia*
D. Blichasz *Northeast*
Philip Brady *West Philadelphia*
Miffy Bright *Washington Square West*
Jean Cacia *South Philadelphia*
Bob Carbonetta *Pennsport*
Nola Castellano *South Philadelphia*
Yevkine Chilingerian *Center City*
Barbara Cilione *South Philadelphia*
Jules Cohen *Queen Village*
Ronnie Colcher *Rittenhouse Square*
Dot DePre *Pennsport*
Jennifer DeRusso *Pennsport*
Stella Davis *Germantown*
Ineka Dikland *Head House Square*
Mirrella DiPalma *Girard Estates*
Cherna Edelman *Art Museum*

Susan Edwards *Fairmount*
Quentin Esmonde *Manayunk*
George Favuzzi *South Philadelphia*
Joyce Fisfis *Northeast*
Susanne Foo *Center City*
Arlene Foster *Manayunk*
John Gangloff *Andorra*
Terry Garrard *University City*
Ki Ko Ko Guiraud
  Washigton Square West
Helen Gorka *Queen Village*
Joanne Graber *Fishtown*
Rose Guarrera *Rittenhouse Square*
Edward Hales *Art Museum*
Patricia Hales *Art Museum*
Rose Hagopian *Center City*
Robert Harmer *Roxsborough*
Linda Harris *Society Hill*
Mary Hayn *Pennsport*
Cyd Hirisch *Washington Square West*
Connie Ippolito *South Philadelphia*
Rose Ippolito *South Philadelphia*
Margaret H. Johnson *Spring Garden*
Sis Johnson *Schuylkill*
Maurie Kerigan *Schuylkill*

ACKNOWLEDGMENTS

Sue Kirscbaum *Chestnut Hill*
Casie Kolatosz *Whitman*
Dolores & William Krupinski
 Foxchase
Tae Kwon *Germantown*
Joshphine LaSpada
 South Philadelphia
Carmen Lebron *Fairhill*
Marge Logan *Schuylkill*
Ilidio F. Lopez *Olney*
Mary Moran *Schuylkill*
Mordecai Matityahu *Northeast*
Eleanor McCrane *Schuylkill*
Marlene McKenzie *Foxchase*
Arnold Miller *Bustleton*
Ivonne Miranda *Logan*
Joan Monica *Foxchase*
Mei Ling Moy *China Town*
Kathy Nace *Manayunk*
Rhoe Nicoletti *Chestnut Hill*
Judith Novey *Fairmount*
Manus Ouathasarn *University City*
Rita Palaia *Frankford*
Suzi Pattison *Society Hill*
Evelyn Perri *South Philadelphia*
Anh Phungly *South Philadelphia*
Alfreda Plocha *Port Richmond*
Joan Putney *Society Hill*
Isabelle Pelullera *Fairhill*
Richard Rest *Art Museum*

Debbie & Bill Richards
 Spring Garden
Rosa Rodriguez *Kensington*
Ruthie Rodriguez *Olney*
Sally Schubert *Mayfair*
Swedish Museum *Packer Park*
Thelma Serbin *Manayunk*
Pat Silva *Chestnut Hill*
Rose Snyder *Northeast*
Iris Stoll *Queen Village*
Sally Solomon *Center City*
Gretle Somerville
 Strawberry Mansion
Mary St. Claire *Center City*
S. H. Stone *Germantown*
Felicity Taormina
 Washington Square West
Adelaide Thomas *Kensington*
Jonathan Turner *Society Hill*
Frank Trautz *Olney*
Despina Vathis *Northeast*
Julie Van de Graaf *Queen Village*
Fred & Pat Voight *Chestnut Hill*
Erika Waginger *Northern Liberties*
Carol Wagner *Society Hill*
Maryanne Walsh *Fishtown*
Mary Waugh *Fishtown*
Kevin Weinsteiger *Northern Liberties*
Jeannette Werner *Fishtown*

Appetizers

Chia-Tzu
Pork Dumplings

From Center City   Chinese   *Makes about 4 dozen*

In a pinch, already made dumpling skins are available at Oriental food shops. However, if you have the time, it is worthwhile making your own.

DOUGH
2 cups sifted all-purpose flour
3/4 cup cold water

FILLING
1 pound lean boneless pork,
  finely ground
1 teaspoon finely chopped
  ginger root
1/4 cup finely chopped scallions
3 tablespoons soy sauce
1/2 teaspoon salt
1 tablespoon sesame oil
1/2 pound Chinese cabbage,
  finely chopped

SAUCE
1/4 cup soy sauce
2 tablespoons white vinegar
1 very thin slice ginger root,
  shredded

Vegetable oil for frying
  dumplings

1. To make the dough, mix the flour with 1/2 cup of the water, adding more water as needed to form a ball. If dough is too sticky, add more flour. Knead the dough until smooth. Put the dough in a bowl, cover with plastic wrap and allow to rest for 30 minutes.

2. Prepare filling. In a large bowl, combine the ground pork, ginger root, scallions, soy sauce, salt and sesame oil. Mix well. Add the chopped cabbage and mix all the ingredients together thoroughly. Reserve.

3. Prepare sauce. Combine all ingredients thoroughly. Reserve.

4. Turn the dough out onto a lightly floured surface. Divide into 2 parts and shape each into a sausage-like cylinder about 12 inches long and 1 inch in diameter. With a sharp knife, cut the rolls crosswise into 1/2-inch slices. Using a rolling pin, roll each slice into a 3-inch round shape about 1/8-inch thick. Repeat with remaining slices.

5. Place 2 teaspoons of filling in center of round and fold in half to form a half moon. To seal, pinch together at the center along the edges. Starting at one end, with your forefinger and thumb, make 2 or 3 pleats on the back side, then pinch them together with the front side of the dough to seal. Pleat and pinch until the opening is completely closed. Repeat with remaining dough and filling. (The dumplings can be prepared and frozen before cooking. Arrange dumplings about 1/8-inch apart on a cookie sheet and freeze. After they are frozen, transfer them to a plastic bag and seal tightly. Drop frozen dumplings into boiling water to cook. Double the cooking time for frozen dumplings.)

6. In a 10-inch skillet, heat 1 tablespoon oil until hot. Place 12-15 dumplings in skillet and add 1/4 cup cold water. Cover, reduce heat to medium and cook for 12-15 minutes, or until all the water has evaporated and the bottom of the dumplings have browned.

7. Carefully remove the dumplings from the pan and serve with the sauce.

Rolled Smoked Seafood Mousse
with Lemon Mayonnaise

From Washington Square West   *Serves 4*

A very elegant yet inexpensive first course that can be made ahead.

4 ounces scallops

4 ounces monkfish

2 ounces smoked white fish

1 teaspoon salt

1/4 teaspoon freshly ground
white pepper

1 tablespoon cognac

3 tablespoons heavy cream

2 egg whites

1/4 pound sea crab in large
pieces

Water

Salad greens herbs (garnish)

LEMON MAYONNAISE

2 egg yolks

3 tablespoons fresh lemon juice

1/4 teaspoon white pepper

1/2 teaspoon salt

3/4-1 cup vegetable oil

1. In a food processor or blender, process the scallops, monkfish and smoked fish until fluffy and smooth. With the processor running, add all the seasonings, cognac, heavy cream and egg whites. Continue processing until the mixture is very smooth and light.

2. Place a double layer of plastic wrap on the counter. Place half the mousse mixture down the center, then place pieces of the sea crab in a line down the middle. Spread the remaining mousse over the sea crab.

3. Bring the plastic wrap up and over the mousse and roll so it is shaped like a long cylinder. Make sure the mousse is completely covered. Tie the ends tightly with twist ties. Smooth the roll gently all over to remove any air bubbles.

4. Poach gently in simmering water for 10 minutes. Turn over and poach another 15 minutes. Allow to cool in the plastic wrap. Slice into 1/2-inch rounds, arrange on a plate and garnish with salad greens and herbs. Serve with lemon mayonnaise.

5. To prepare lemon mayonnaise, whisk together the egg yolks, lemon juice and seasonings in a food processor or blender. Slowly pour in the oil until the mayonnaise is light and creamy. It should not be as thick as a regular mayonnaise.

Deviled Clams

From Queen Village *Serves 8-10*

The large cherrystone clams are best to use for this recipe. Although this dish has several stages of preparation, the end result is worth it. They are succulent, crispy and delicious.

3-4 dozen large clams, scrubbed, cleaned and thoroughly rinsed of sand

Butter for greasing clam shells

2 tablespoons vegetable oil

4 green peppers, very finely diced

4 celery stalks, very finely diced

4 onions, minced

3 garlic cloves, minced

1 teaspoon cayenne pepper

Pinch of salt

3 cups bread crumbs

2 eggs, beaten

1/4 cup milk

Vegetable oil for frying

1. Put the clams in a large pot, cover tightly and steam them open over high heat. Move the clams around in the pot with a spatula from time to time. Some clams may take longer than others to open. Discard any clams that do not open at all. Reserve broth. Pull out the clam meat from the shell and mince.

2. Separate the shells in two. Butter them all over and refrigerate

3. In a skillet, heat the 2 tablespoons of oil and sauté the peppers, celery, onions and garlic until soft, approximately 2-3 minutes. Add a little of the reserved clam broth just to moisten the vegetables. Add the cayenne pepper and salt, then stir. Add the minced clams and about 1/3 cup of bread crumbs, just enough to hold the filling together. Mix gently. Refrigerate 1 hour.

4. Remove clam shells and filling from refrigerator and fill the shells generously.

5. Mix the beaten egg and milk together in a bowl. Place the bread crumbs in a separate dish. Dip the filled clam shell into the bread crumbs, then into the egg/milk mixture and coat all over once more with bread crumbs.

6. In a pan, heat the oil and deep-fry the clams for 4-5 minutes or until they are nicely browned. Serve immediately.

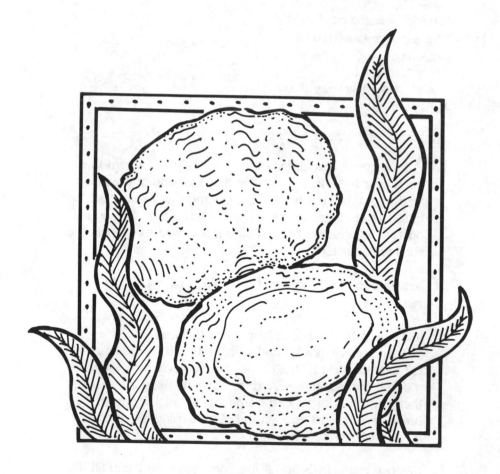

Vongole a Forno
Broiled Clams on the Half Shell

From Rittenhouse Square   **Italian**   *Serves 6*

These make wonderful hors d'oeuvres. The littleneck clams are very sweet and delectable.

2 dozen littleneck clams, scrubbed clean, opened and on the half shell

1 cup fresh bread crumbs

2 tablespoons finely chopped Italian parsley

2 garlic cloves, finely chopped

1/2 teaspoon basil

1/2 teaspoon oregano

Salt and pepper to taste

Red pepper flakes to taste

1 tablespoon olive oil, or more if necessary

1. In a bowl, combine the bread crumbs, parsley, garlic, basil, oregano, salt and pepper and red pepper flakes to taste. Moisten mixture with olive oil. (Add just enough oil to bind mixture together.)

2. Top each clam with a little of the bread crumb mixture and cook under the broiler for 3-4 minutes or until golden brown. Serve at once.

Baccala Fritto
Codfish Fritters

From South Philadelphia   **Italian**   *Makes 24 fritters*

These very traditional Italian fritters are light and tasty. Baccala is available pre-soaked which saves preparation time.

1 pound baccala, soaked in water to cover (refrigerate for 2-3 days, changing the water frequently; drain well)

1 cup flour

1 egg, lightly beaten

Pepper to taste

1/2 cup milk or just enough to make a thick batter

Oil for frying

Horseradish/sour cream sauce (page 219)

1. In boiling water, blanch the prepared baccala for 2 minutes. Drain and shred finely.

2. In a bowl, add the shredded baccala, flour, egg and pepper, mix well. Slowly add the milk, enough so it makes a thick batter.

3. Heat oil in a skillet, approximately 2 inches deep. Drop spoonfuls of baccala mixture into the hot oil. Cook until golden in color, turning over once or twice. Drain on paper towels and serve with horseradish/sour cream sauce.

Ki Ku Ko
Salmon Rolls

From Washington Square West   **Japanese**   *Makes 8 rolls*

A quick and easy do-ahead appetizer. The daikon adds a fresh peppery taste that is sure to please the palate.

8 thinly sliced pieces of smoked salmon

1/2 cup julienne strips of daikon (giant white radish)

Watercress

MUSTARD-SOY DRESSING

1/4 cup mustard with seeds

1 teaspoon vegetable oil

1/2 teaspoon lemon juice

1/4 teaspoon light soy sauce, or to taste

1. Place a few strips of daikon and watercress sprigs on top of smoked salmon pieces and roll securely.

2. Prepare mustard-soy dressing. In a small bowl, whisk the ingredients together. Serve with rolls.

Gravad Lax
Marinated Salmon

From the Swedish Museum,   **Swedish**   *Serves 4-6*
Packer Park

Dill is often used in pickling fish and is traditionally used in many Scandinavian dishes. A good dry champagne enhances this dish for a special occasion. This can be served as a light lunch with buttered new potatoes and a tossed salad.

2 salmon fillets, about 1-2 pounds each	**DILL DRESSING**
1/2 cup salt	3 tablespoons olive oil
1/4 cup sugar	1 1/2 teaspoons vinegar
4-5 sprigs of dill	1 tablespoon Dijon mustard
10 white peppercorns, crushed	Dill, chopped
	Salt and pepper to taste

1. In a bowl, mix the salt, sugar and pepper together. Rub thoroughly into both pieces of salmon.

2. Place one of the fillets in a dish large enough so it fits comfortably. Place sprigs of dill on top, then cover with second salmon fillet, skin side up.

3. Cover with wax paper and place a heavy weight on top. Refrigerate for 1-2 days, turning the fish over once a day.

4. Prepare dill dressing. Whisk together all the ingredients. Add lots of dill.

5. Before serving salmon, remove the dill sprigs from the fillets and scrape off any of the seasonings. Cut into medium slices and serve with dressing.

Nacho a la Reste

From Art Museum Area   *Serves 8-10*

A hearty, heavy-duty appetizer with a festive flair. Great with margaritas!

1 16-ounce can refried beans

2 cups Monterey Jack cheese, grated

1 pound ground beef, browned and well drained of fat

1 4-ounce can chopped green chilies

1 4-ounce can taco sauce

2 avocados, mashed with 1 teaspoon lemon juice

1/2 cup chopped green onions

1 cup sour cream

Tortilla chips

---

1. Preheat oven to 350°.

2. In a saucepan, heat the refried beans with 1 cup of the cheese, until cheese melts.

3. Layer the beans, browned beef, chilies, remaining cheese and taco sauce in a 12-inch oven-proof platter or casserole. Place in oven for about 15 minutes or until heated through.

4. Remove from oven and spread on the mashed avocado, most of the green onions and the sour cream. Garnish with remaining green onions. Serve with tortilla chips.

Shrimp and Cheese Mousse

From Art Museum Area   *Serves 8*

This short-cut version of a "mousse" is excellent for a make-ahead appetizer.

1 11-ounce can condensed tomato soup

6 ounces cream cheese

1 cup mayonnaise (homemade, page 214)

1 1/2 tablespoons (1 1/2 packets) gelatin

1/4 cup clam or shrimp juice

1 1/4 cups finely chopped celery

1/4 cup finely chopped onion

2 4 1/4-ounce cans baby shrimp, chopped

Tabasco sauce, a few drops to taste

1. In a medium-size saucepan, boil the tomato soup without adding water. Remove from heat and stir in the cream cheese until melted.

2. Mix the gelatin into the clam juice to dissolve and add to the mixture.

3. Stir in the remaining ingredients and pour into a greased 8-cup mold or 8 1/2-cup individual ramekins. Chill in refrigerator to set. Unmold to serve.

Serving suggestion: Serve with cocktail pumpernickle bread or crackers.

Tri-Cheese Dip

From Fitler Square   ***Makes about 2 cups***

Try using other combinations of cheeses such as brie mixed together with Boursin pepper cheese.

1 8-ounce package of cream cheese, at room temperature

1/4 pound creamy blue cheese

2 ounces Boursin garlic cheese

1 tablespoon horseradish

Parsley or paprika (garnish)

1. Combine all the above ingredients in a blender or food processor and whiz until very smooth.

2. Put into a serving bowl and garnish with parsley or sprinkle with a little paprika, if desired.

Serving suggestion: Serve with a selection of crackers or variety of raw vegetables.

Hot Crab Dip

From Chestnut Hill   *Makes about 1-1 1/2 cups*

This is a wonderful party dish with lots of flavor. Serve also for a light luncheon dish on toast tips with just a tossed salad. If possible, use freshly grated horseradish for a more pronounced flavor.

8 ounces cream cheese, softened

1/2 pound crabmeat, fresh or frozen (if using fresh, pick through crabmeat for cartilage)

1 tablespoon horseradish, more or less to taste

1/2 teaspoon salt

1/3 cup butter or margarine, softened

3 tablespoons minced onion

1/2 cup slivered almonds, toasted

1. Preheat oven to 375°.

2. Whiz all the above ingredients except almonds in a food processor or blender, or combine thoroughly in a bowl.

3. Pour into an oven-proof dish and sprinkle with toasted almonds.

4. Bake for 15 minutes or until heated through.

Serving suggestion: Serve with crackers, cocktail-size rye bread, or melba toast.

Beet Dip

From Art Museum Area   ***Makes 1-2 cups***

A colorful and unusual dip that is easy to make and has a very refreshing flavor.

1/2 cup of canned beets, drained (do not use pickled beets)

6 ounces cream cheese

1 tablespoon minced onion

2 teaspoons red wine vinegar

1/4 teaspoon salt

1/4 teaspoon Tabasco sauce

1. Place ingredients in a blender or food processor.

2. Blend until very smooth, scraping the bowl down occasionally.

Serving suggestion: Serve with assorted raw vegetables such as broccoli, snowpeas, mushrooms, cauliflower or asparagus spears.

Captain's Table Avocado Dip

From Belmont   *Makes about 2 cups*

The crab adds richness to this avocado dip and is always a favorite at parties. Either salted or unsalted roasted macadamia nuts can be used. They add a crunchy, slightly sweet flavor to this recipe.

2 medium avocados

Juice of half a lemon

1 tablespoon brandy

2 tablespoons tomato sauce

1 tablespoon horseradish sauce

1 cup heavy cream

Salt and pepper to taste

1/2 pound fresh crab meat, picked over for cartilage

Lettuce leaves (garnish)

Macadamia nuts, chopped (garnish)

Parsley, chopped, (garnish)

1. Scoop out flesh of avocado and put into a blender or food processor. Add the lemon juice, brandy, tomato sauce and horseradish and blend or process until smooth. Turn into a bowl and gradually add the cream, salt and pepper. Stir until well mixed.

2. Fold the crab into the above mixture.

3. Serve cold in individual glass dishes lined with lettuce leaves. Sprinkle with chopped macadamia nuts and chopped parsley.

Serving suggestion: This is a very elegant presentation for a first course or to serve as hors d'oeuvres.

Layered Spicy Avocado Dip

From Society Hill   ***Makes 3-4 cups***

In order to bring out the subtle taste of the spices in this Tex-Mex dip, it should be made in advance so that all the spices blend well. Bring to room temperature before serving.

FIRST LAYER

3 medium soft avocados, peeled and cubed

2 tablespoons white vinegar

1 4-ounce can green chilies

Salt and pepper to taste

(Mix all ingredients together in blender or food processor and place on the bottom of a serving bowl.)

SECOND LAYER

1 cup sour cream

1 cup mayonnaise

1 package taco seasoning

(Mix ingredients together and pour on top of the avocado mixture.)

THIRD LAYER

1 cup chopped scallions

1 cup black olives, pitted and sliced

1 cup shredded cheese (Cheddar and Monterey Jack)

3 tomatoes, chopped

(Mix ingredients together and sprinkle on top of second layer.)

Serve with tostados or nachos.

Mushroom Tarts

From Queen Village　　　　　　　　***Makes 48 small tarts***

Mushroom tarts can be served at room temperature or heated through. Also they freeze well. To thaw, simply heat filled shells for approximately 12 minutes at 400°.

CRUST
2 1/2 cups flour, sifted with 1/2 teaspoon salt
2/3 cup sweet butter
1/3 cup sour cream
1 egg, lightly beaten

FILLING
1/4 cup sweet butter
1/4 pound mushrooms, finely chopped
2 tablespoons finely chopped green onions
1/4 cup flour
1/2 teaspoon salt
1 cup heavy whipping cream

1. Preheat oven to 400°.

2. In a large bowl or food processor, add the flour and cut in the butter. Add the sour cream and egg and mix until thoroughly blended.

3. Using about 1 teaspoon of dough, form a ball. Using your fingers, press the dough in the bottom and up the sides of tiny tart shells about 1 3/4 inches in diameter. (Larger tart shells can be used if preferred.)

4. Bake the shells for 12-15 minutes or until golden.

5. To make the filling, first melt the butter in a skillet. Add the mushrooms and onions and cook for 1-2 minutes. Stir in the flour and salt. Add the whipping cream and cook, stirring constantly, until thick and smooth. Fill pastry shells with mushroom mixture.

Stuffed Mushrooms

From Art Museum Area **Serves 4**

With beautiful white cultivated mushrooms so readily available, these can be enjoyed all year round. They can also be served as a side vegetable with steak or chops.

16 large mushrooms, wiped clean with a damp paper towel

Olive oil for baking sheet

1/4 cup grated Monterey Jack cheese

1/4 cup grated Cheddar

1 tablespoon Italian flavored bread crumbs

1/2 small onion, grated

Salt and pepper to taste

4 tablespoons butter

1. Preheat oven to 325°.

2. Remove mushroom stems. Reserve them for another use. Place the cleaned mushroom caps on a lightly oiled baking sheet.

3. Mix together the cheeses, bread crumbs, onion, salt and pepper to taste.

4. Fill the caps with the mixture. Put a dot of butter on top of each cap and cook in oven for about 10-15 minutes, or until the cheese has melted.

Variation: Mince the mushroom stems, adding a few extra caps. Sauté the minced mushrooms with 4 finely chopped scallions in 2 tablespoons butter and 1 tablespoon olive oil. Season with thyme, parsley, garlic powder, salt and pepper to taste. Add enough bread crumbs to bind together. Fill caps, dot with butter and bake at 375° for 10-15 minutes.

Funghi Marinati
Marinated Mushrooms

From South Philadelphia   **Italian**   *Serves 6-8*

This method of simmering the mushrooms in the marinade brings out a more concentrated earthy flavor which you will find absolutely delicious.

1 pound mushrooms, wiped
  clean, stem tips removed
2 cups white wine vinegar
1/2 cup diced celery
2 garlic cloves, sliced

2 teaspoons oregano
Salt and pepper to taste
1-2 cups olive oil, enough to
  cover mushrooms

1. In a saucepan, bring white wine vinegar to a boil. Add mushrooms and simmer 3-4 minutes. Drain, reserving 1 tablespoon vinegar.

2. In a bowl, add celery, garlic, oregano, salt, pepper and mushrooms. Cover with oil plus the reserved tablespoon vinegar. Marinate overnight.

Serving suggestion: These savory mushrooms can be served as a first course on a bed of crisp lettuce or as hors d'oeuvres with cocktail toothpicks.

Chá Ctīo
Spring Rolls

From South Philadelphia   **Vietnamese**   *Makes about 24 rolls*

The secret of these wonderfully crispy, golden glazed spring rolls is the egg used to brush each rice paper triangle. They are as eye-appealing as they are delicious.

1 pound ground lean pork

1 large onion, finely chopped

4 ounces cellophane noodles* (soaked in warm water 3 minutes, then cut into 1-inch pieces)

2 ounces wood-ears* (soaked in warm water 15 minutes, cleaned and finely chopped)

1 teaspoon salt

1/2 teaspoon black pepper

2 tablespoons fish sauce*

1 tablespoon dry sherry

4 extra large eggs

1/2 pound fresh bean sprouts

8 large rice paper circles*

Soybean oil* for deep-frying (approximately 2 cups)

NUOC CHAM SAUCE

1/2 cup fish sauce*

1 1/2 cups water

5 teaspoons vinegar

1/4-1/2 cup sugar

1/4 cup grated carrot

1 teaspoon chili pepper flakes

1. Prepare nuoc cham sauce. Combine all ingredients until well blended. Set aside.

2. To make filling, combine pork, onion, noodles, wood-ears, salt, pepper, fish sauce and sherry. Lightly beat 1 of the eggs and add to mixture. Mix in bean sprouts.

3. Cut each rice paper circle into 3-inch pie-shaped wedges. Beat remaining 3 eggs and brush each triangle with egg before adding filling. Place 2-3 tablespoons of filling on each triangle at the pointed end. Fold end over filling, fold sides in, then roll firmly. Press edges together to seal.

4. Heat oil to 350° for deep frying. Fry rolls a few at a time until lightly browned and filling cooks through, about 12 minutes. Drain on paper towels. Serve with nuoc cham sauce.

Variation: Garlic and chopped shrimp may be added to filling, if desired. (*Available at Oriental food stores.)

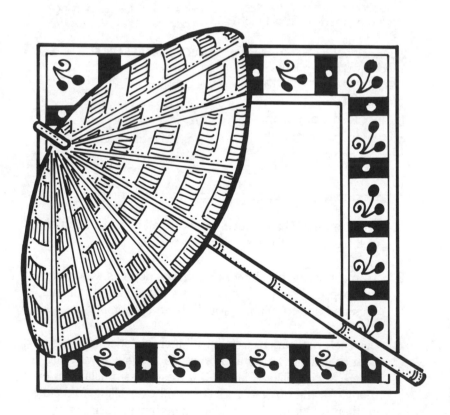

Sausage Pinwheels

From Rittenhouse Square   ***Makes about 60 pinwheels***

These sausage pinwheels can be made as spicy or mild as you like by altering the amount of hot to sweet sausage. They can be prepared ahead, frozen and heated when needed.

1 pound hot Italian sausage

1 pound sweet Italian sausage

1 package frozen puff pastry, thawed

1 egg, beaten with 1 tablespoon water for egg wash

1. Remove sausage from casing. Place in a skillet and sauté, breaking up lumps of sausage as they fry. Drain well in a colander to remove excess fat. If sausage is not broken into fine pieces, place in food processor or blender and whiz once or twice. Cool completely.

2. Preheat oven to 425°.

3. Cut each piece of puff pastry in half. Roll to about 9 x 15 inches. Spread sausage evenly over the surface and roll tightly in a jelly-roll fashion. Cut into 3/4-inch pieces. Seal end of rounds with egg wash. Repeat process with remaining sheets of puff pastry. With a pastry brush, brush egg wash on top and sides of pinwheels. (Egg wash will give a shiny golden color to pinwheels when baked.)

4. Bake on an ungreased cookie sheet for approximately 20 minutes or until lightly browned.

Bánh Khóai Húê
Happy Pancakes

From South Philadelphia   **Vietnamese**   *Serves 6*

In Vietnamese, the words for "happy" and "sound" are similar. Originally the "happy pancake" was referred to as "sound cake" because of the sound made as the ingredients were placed in the very hot, sputtering oil. These Happy Pancakes are truly delicious and will bring much pleasure when served.

1/2 pound rice flour*

2 cups water

1 scallion, cleaned, trimmed and finely chopped

1 large egg

Soybean oil* (approximately 2 cups) for frying pancakes

3/4 pound small shrimp, shelled and deveined

3/4 pound uncooked chicken or pork, thinly sliced

1/4 pound mushrooms, thinly sliced

1 large onion, thinly sliced

1/2 pound fresh bean sprouts

FISH SAUCE
1 cup bottled fish sauce*

3 tablespoons vinegar

3 cups water

1/2 cup sugar

1 cup grated carrot

1 teaspoon dried chili pepper

1. Prepare fish sauce. In a bowl, blend all ingredients thoroughly. Reserve.

2. To make the pancakes, combine rice flour, water, scallion and egg. Blend well.

3. Have the prepared shrimp, chicken or pork, mushrooms, onion and bean sprouts close at hand for adding to pancakes.

4. In a medium-size skillet, add 5 tablespoons soybean oil and heat until hot. Add one-sixth of the shrimp, chicken, mushrooms and onion to the pan and stir-fry over high heat until lightly cooked, but not brown, about 3 minutes. Oil should be bubbling.

5. Add one-sixth of the batter to the skillet and spread with one-sixth of the bean sprouts. Cover pan, lower heat to medium and cook until edges begin to brown. Loosen bottom of pancake with a spatula and fold over like an omelet. Drain on paper towel. Repeat 5 more times with remaining ingredients. Serve with fish sauce.

*Available at Oriental food stores.

Lašqnočia
Ham and Bacon Rolls

From Port Richmond   **Lithuanian**   *Makes 15-20 rolls*

These traditional Lithuanian favorites are time-consuming but well worth the effort. They are very delicious and can be made ahead and frozen.

1/4 cup warm water

1 package yeast

1/2 teaspoon sugar

1/4 pound (1 stick) butter

1 cup milk

1 egg and 1 egg yolk, beaten together

1 cup water

1 teaspoon salt

2 tablespoons sugar

6-7 cups flour

4-6 cups ham, finely chopped

3/4 pound bacon, diced

2 medium onions, finely chopped

Freshly ground black pepper

1 egg white and 1 tablespoon water

1. In a bowl, place the warm water, yeast and sugar together. Mix gently to dissolve, cover and let stand in a warm place for 5 minutes to proof.

2. Meanwhile, melt the butter and pour into a large bowl. Add the milk, beaten egg, water, salt and sugar, together with the proofed yeast. Gradually add the flour, mixing with a wooden spoon. You will probably use about 5-6 cups of flour. The dough will be a little sticky. Gather into the middle of the bowl, cover and let sit for about 1-1 1/2 hours or until it has doubled in size.

3. Spread the remaining flour on the table and knead the raised dough for about 5 minutes, adding more flour if necessary. The texture of the dough should be fairly soft. Set aside again in the bowl, cover and let rise for about 1 hour or until double in size.

4. While the dough is rising, you can prepare the filling. In a skillet, fry the bacon until fairly crisp, remove and place in a bowl together with the diced ham. In the same skillet, fry the onions until lightly browned and add them also to the chopped ham and bacon. Remove from heat and add a little black pepper.

5. Preheat oven to 400°.

6. Roll out the dough about 1/8-inch thick. Cut into circles of about 3-3 1/3 inches. Place a small spoonful of filling on one side, fold over and pinch the dough together. Place on a lightly oiled baking sheet, brush with the egg white that has been beaten with 1 tablespoon water. Bake for about 20 minutes.

Variation: Roll the dough out flat, place the filling down the center. Roll and bake. This makes a very tasty bread to serve with soups or as an appetizer.

Chicken Wings with Oyster Sauce

From Chinatown   **Chinese**   *Serves 4*

Here is an easy chicken dish that makes an excellent hors d'oeuvre. The main flavor comes from the dark brown oyster sauce, which is made from an extract of whole oysters.

10-12 chicken wings   2 tablespoons soy sauce
1 slice fresh ginger   1 tablespoon dry sherry
Vegetable oil for frying wings   1/2 teaspoon sugar
3-4 tablespoons oyster sauce*   1 cup water

1. Divide chicken wings into 2 pieces by separating the large joint from the v-shaped piece.

2. In a wok or large skillet, add ginger slice and enough oil to cover bottom of pan and heat until hot. Brown the wings (cook half at a time so as not to overcrowd skillet.)

3. Pour out excess oil and discard ginger slice. Add all remaining ingredients to wok or skillet, cover and simmer 10 minutes. Remove lid and cook another 10-15 minutes, or until wings are tender and sauce is reduced. During cooking, baste wings frequently with sauce. When done, wings should be coated with a heavy glaze of sauce.

*Available at many supermarkets and at Oriental and specialty food shops.

Chicken Wing-Dings with Spicy Sauce

From Port Richmond   *Serves 4*

An unusual preparation for chicken wings. Serve with plenty of napkins.

12-15 chicken wings (cut tip portion off, cut wing part in 2 pieces)

2 eggs

1/4 cup milk

1 cup seasoned bread crumbs

1/2 tablespoon Italian seasoning

1/2 tablespoon Old Bay seasoning

1 cup flour

Salt and pepper

Oil for frying

1. In a dish, mix the eggs and milk together.

2. On another plate, mix the bread crumbs, Italian seasoning and Old Bay seasoning.

3. Use a third plate for the flour and season with salt and pepper.

4. Dredge the wings first in the flour, shake off excess flour. Dip into egg/milk mixture and finally coat with the bread crumbs.

5. Heat the oil in a large saucepan or fryer. Deep-fry the wings until golden, about 4-5 minutes. Drain and serve with spicy barbecue sauce (page 216).

Formaggio Fritto
Cheese Fritters

From Andorra   **Italian**   *Makes about 15 fritters*

These fritters are usually accompanied by an Italian aperatif or a good dry white wine.

1 8-ounce package
mozzarella (Bel Paese or
Parmesan cheese can be
substituted)

Grated Parmesan cheese

3 eggs, separated

2 tablespoons flour

1/2 teaspoon salt

Black pepper or cayenne to
taste

Oil for frying

1. Half fill a deep saucepan with oil and heat until hot.

2. Cut the mozzarella into small pieces. In a blender or food processor beat the egg yolks, add the cheese and blend until evenly distributed. Add the flour, salt and pepper and mix again.

3. Beat the egg whites until stiff, then lightly fold in the cheese mixture.

4. Take a tablespoon and scoop up some of the mixture, then scrape the batter off with the tip of a knife into the hot oil. Cook until lightly browned, turning once or twice.

5. Drain on paper towels and serve, sprinkled with a little Parmesan cheese.

Pierogi

From Queen Village   **Polish**   *Makes about 3 1/2 dozen*

Pierogi are wonderful served as finger-food at cocktail parties or as a luncheon entrée. The prune-filled pierogi are traditionally served at Christmas Eve dinner.

DOUGH
3 cups flour
1 egg
1 teaspoon oil
1/2 cup milk
1/2 cup water
1/2 teaspoon salt

CHEESE FILLING (fills about 3 1/2 dozen pierogi)
2 pounds dry cottage cheese (farmer's cheese or pot-style)
2 eggs
1/4 teaspoon ground cinnamon
1/2 teaspoon salt
4 tablespoons sugar

(Mix all above ingredients together.)

POTATO FILLING (fills about 3 dozen pierogi)
1 1/2 pounds mashed potatoes
1 small onion, minced and sautéed in butter
1/4 cup shredded cheese (Monterey Jack, Swiss, American)
Salt and pepper to taste

(Mix all above ingredients together.)

MUSHROOM FILLING (fills about 3 dozen pierogi)
1 pound mushrooms, wiped clean and finely chopped
1-2 tablespoons butter or margarine
1 small onion, minced
1 stick celery, minced
Plain bread crumbs
Salt and pepper to taste

(In a frying pan, heat butter and saute onion and celery until soft. Add finely chopped mushrooms and cook another 10-15 minutes. Cool filling and add enough bread crumbs to absorb butter. Salt and pepper to taste.)

BLUEBERRY FILLING (fills about 2 1/2 dozen pierogi)
1 pint blueberries, rinsed
2 tablespoons sugar
1 tablespoon lemon juice
1 tablespoon cornstarch or flour

(Mix all above ingredients together.)

CABBAGE FILLINGS (fills 2 1/2-3 dozen pierogi)

1 small head of cabbage, quartered and cooked in water 15 minutes, drained and chopped

1 small onion, minced and sautéed in 4 tablespoons butter

1/2 teaspoon salt

1/4 teaspoon pepper

(Mix all above ingredients together.)

PRUNE FILLING (fills about 2 1/2 dozen pierogi)

1 pound pitted dried prunes

(In a bowl, cover prunes with hot water and leave overnight. Drain and dry completely. Place 1 prune in each pierogi.)

---

1. To make dough: On a table or flat surface, mix all ingredients together and knead into a soft dough. (Push aside about 1/3 cup of the original 3 cups flour and add gradually as you knead and roll to prevent sticking.)

2. Roll out half the dough at a time to about 1/4-inch thickness. Using a glass or cup about 3 1/2 inches in diameter, press out circles of dough.

3. Place about 1 tablespoon of filling on dough circle, pressing it flat against the center. Fold over and press edges together firmly, sealing them with a little water. Flute edges, pressing dough between thumb and forefinger, or seal with tines of a fork. (Pierogi seal better when you fill the side that was rolled against the table as it stays moister than the top side.) Pat filled pierogi with flour and place on paper towels.

4. To cook, drop into boiling water and stir gently so that pierogi do not stick to the pot or to each other. Bring water back to a boil and cook pierogi for 4-5 minutes. Lift out gently with a slotted spoon and place in a colander. Drain and cover each batch with melted butter. Serve with additional melted butter and/or sour cream.

Variation: Boiled pierogi can also be sautéed in a small amount of butter until lightly golden on both sides.

Soups and Stocks

Basic Chicken Stock

From Oxford Circle   ***Makes about 4 cups***

Chicken stock can also be made from the water in which you braise a whole chicken. When chicken is cooked, shred the meat and use as you wish. Return bones to the water and continue simmering for another 1-2 hours. Strain and cool.

4 pounds chicken bones, necks, wings and giblets

1 veal bone (optional)

1 onion

2 celery ribs

1 carrot

5 black peppercorns

Water

1. Place all the above ingredients into a large stock pot. Cover with water and bring to a boil. Lower heat and simmer for 2-3 hours.

2. Strain the stock through a cheesecloth-lined colander. Cool and refrigerate or freeze. If not using for 2 to 3 days, bring to a boil again for a few minutes and then use.

Basic Fish Stock

From Wynnefield   ***Makes 8-9 cups***

Fish stock should be brought to a boil once a day until used. It should not be refrigerated for more than 3 days. Stock may also be frozen until needed.

3-4 pounds fish head bones

2 leeks, cleaned and sliced

1 onion, peeled and sliced

1 bay leaf

6 sprigs parsley

1/2 teaspoon whole black peppercorns

3 cups dry white wine dry

Enough water to cover the fish bones

1. Chop the bones into fairly large pieces and place in a stock pot. Add the leeks, onions, bay leaf, parsley, whole black peppercorns and white wine. Cover the fish with water to an inch above the bones.

2. Simmer uncovered for 30 minutes.

3. Strain the stock through a cheesecloth-lined colander. Allow to cool and then refrigerate until needed or freeze.

Zuppa di Cozze
Mussel Soup

From Manayunk   **Italian**   *Serves 4*

Mussels are a great delicacy and in their shiny blue-black shells are always spectacular in any dish. Mussels must be well scrubbed and any open raw mussels should be discarded.

24 mussels

1 tablespoon baking soda for cleaning mussels

1 tablespoon olive oil

2-3 garlic cloves, chopped

2 cups white wine

2 cups tomato sauce (page 220)

---

1. In a large bowl, soak the mussels in cold water and sprinkle with 1 tablespoon of baking soda for about 1 hour. This helps to release the sand from the mussels. Lift mussels out with a slotted spoon, scrub well and pull off the beard.

2. In a large pot, add the oil and garlic, cook until lightly browned. Do not burn.

3. Add the mussels, cover the pot and steam until the shells open. Discard any unopened mussels.

4. Add the white wine and tomato sauce. Simmer for 4-5 minutes.

Serving suggestion: This is also delicious served as a sauce over pasta.

Cream of Shrimp Soup

From Center City   ***Makes 4 cups or 2 bowls***

A creamy texture and the delicate taste of shrimp make this an outstanding soup.

1/4 pound shrimp with shells
  left on, rinsed under cold
  running water

1/2 cup dry sherry

1/2 cup water

1 small carrot, chopped

1 small onion, sliced

1 small celery stalk with leaves,
  chopped

Sprig of parsley

1 bay leaf

1 garlic clove

Pinch of thyme

10 peppercorns

1 tablespoon butter

1 tablespoon flour

1/2 cup milk

Salt and pepper to taste

1 egg yolk

1/4 cup heavy cream

Butter (garnish)

Parsley (garnish)

1. In a saucepan, combine sherry, water, carrot, onion, celery, parsley, bay leaf, garlic, thyme and peppercorns. Simmer for approximately 10 minutes. Replace water if too much evaporation has taken place.

2. Add shrimp and simmer 5 minutes. Remove shell, devein and chop shrimp. Reserve cooking broth.

3. In another saucepan, cook the butter and flour together for 1-2 minutes. Strain the broth into the butter/flour mixture. Add the milk and season to taste. (More milk may be added to stretch the soup.)

4. In a small bowl, beat the egg yolk. Add the heavy cream and beat. Add a little of the heated broth to the egg yolk mixture to heat and then pour back into the remaining broth. (This helps to neutralize the temperature of the egg yolk mixture and will prevent the egg from cooking.) Add the chopped shrimp and simmer gently. Garnish with a pat of butter and parsley.

Zuppa di Festa
Italian Holiday Soup

From Chestnut Hill   ***Serves 10-12***

This delicious soup is traditionally served at Christmas or Easter. The meatballs add a distinct robust personality to this dish. Any leftovers can be frozen and reheated when desired.

12 cups chicken broth
(preferably homemade)

2 bunches escarole, washed
thoroughly and chopped

4 eggs beaten with 1/2 cup
Parmesan cheese (mix in a
cup with a spout)

MEATBALLS
1 pound ground chuck

3/4 cup bread crumbs

1/4 cup chopped Italian parsley

1 egg

1/2 cup water

1/2 cup grated Parmesan
cheese

Sprinkling of garlic powder

Salt and pepper to taste

1. Prepare meatballs. Combine all ingredients thoroughly by hand and shape into small balls, about 1 inch in diameter.

2. Bring chicken broth to a boil and add chopped escarole. Reduce heat and simmer gently for 5-8 minutes.

3. Drop the meatballs into the broth, a few at a time, and stir gently. Simmer gently for 8-10 minutes.

4. In a thin, steady stream, slowly pour the Parmesan/egg mixture into the simmering broth. Stir and simmer 1 minute.

5. Turn off heat and allow soup to settle for about 10-15 minutes before serving.

"My Grandchildren's Buldig Soup"
Chicken Soup with Meatballs and Noodles

From Overbrook   **Armenian**   *Serves 4*

In this recipe, noodles are added which thicken the soup and turn it into a hearty, delicious meal-in-itself dish.

1 pound ground meat (lean beef or lamb or a combination of both)

Salt and pepper to taste

4 cups chicken broth

1 1/2 cups thick egg noodles

3 teaspoons fresh lemon juice, or to taste

1. Mix the meat with salt and pepper and make small meatballs, about 1/2-inch in diameter.

2. Bring the broth to a boil and put in meatballs. Reduce heat and simmer for about 20 minutes.

3. Add noodles and cook another half hour or more until noodles are done.

4. Before serving, add lemon juice to soup. Adjust seasonings and serve.

Cha Wan Mushi
Steamed Egg Soup

From Washington Square West   **Japanese**   *Serves 4*

This is a typical Japanese egg soup with a consistency of a light custard. The soy sauce adds a light and delicious flavor. Shiitake mushrooms are flat looking with white undersides. If using dried shiitake in this recipe, be sure to soak them for about 20 minutes in warm water until tender.

4 round slices of carrot (or carrot rounds cut with decorative cutter)

4 snow peas

4 pieces fresh shiitake mushrooms*

2 eggs, beaten

4 cups chicken stock (preferably homemade)

1 tablespoon light-colored soy sauce

4 small slices 2x1 inch uncooked chicken, marinated in a small amount of soy sauce

1. In a small saucepan of boiling water, add the carrot rounds, snow peas and shiitake, and cook until vegetables are tender but still crisp, about 5 minutes.

2. In a bowl, place beaten egg, chicken stock and soy sauce. Strain through a fine sieve or strainer.

3. Place one piece of chicken in each of 4 heat-proof bowls. Place in a pot of boiling water (water should come half way up the bowls). Cover pot and cook the chicken over medium high heat, about 3-4 minutes or until just opaque. Lower heat to medium low. Ladle broth into bowls. Cover pot and cook another 5 minutes or until egg in soup has become slightly set.

4. Add snow peas, carrot and mushroom on top. If egg is set adequately, vegetables will float on top. Turn off heat and serve. This soup is especially elegant served in small Japanese soup bowls with lids.

*Available at Oriental food shops.

Dak Kook
Chicken Soup with Clams and Spinach

From Olney   **Korean**   *Serves 4*

A delicate soup with an unusual combination of clams and chicken. Do not overcook the clams or they will toughen.

16 clams, well cleaned

1 tablespoon peanut oil

1 1/2 teaspoons minced fresh ginger

1 garlic clove, minced

3 scallions, chopped

1 boneless chicken breast, skinned and shredded

5 cups chicken stock (preferably homemade)

1 pound fresh spinach, washed and chopped

1 teaspoon sesame oil

---

1. In a large saucepan or wok, heat the oil. Add the ginger, garlic, scallions and chicken. Stir-fry over a high heat for about 30 seconds.

2. Add the chicken stock, bring to a boil, lower heat and simmer for 5 minutes.

3. Add the clams, cover and steam until clam shells open, about 5-8 minutes. Discard any unopened clams.

4. Add the spinach to the soup and cook 1-2 minutes more. Add the sesame oil and serve.

Beef Vegetable Soup

From Queen Village   *Serves 4*

This sturdy soup is rich and hearty and can be prepared ahead. The soup greens called for in this recipe are also known as pot herbs.

3 large beef shanks with bones

1 28-ounce can crushed tomatoes

3 medium onions, coarsely chopped

3 celery stalks, chopped

2 carrots, sliced

1 teaspoon marjoram

1 teaspoon thyme

2 tablespoons soup greens

1 small head cabbage, finely chopped (optional)

1/2 cup barley, medium pearled

1 10-ounce box frozen mixed vegetables

Salt and pepper to taste

1/2 cup elbow macaroni

12-16 German dumplings (optional) (page 167)

---

1. Remove meat from bones and cut into 2-inch square chunks.

2. In a large stockpot, add meat and bones and enough water to cover, about 4 cups. Bring to a boil and skim off residue.

3. Reduce heat to low, add crushed tomatoes, onion, celery and carrot and cook covered for 1 hour.

4. Season with marjoram, thyme, soup greens, salt and pepper. If using cabbage, add at this point. Add the barley and continue cooking another 1 1/2-2 hours.

5. Add frozen mixed vegetables. After 15-20 minutes, add elbow macaroni and cook until elbows are done. If using dumplings, add to soup during the last 10-20 minutes of cooking time. Remove bones before serving.

Tripe Soup

From Oxford Circle   ***Serves 4***

Beef tripe is generally available, but honeycomb tripe is considered the best. Tripe requires a fairly long cooking time to tenderize.

1 1/2 pounds beef honeycomb tripe	1 celery stalk
3 cups water	Salt and pepper
1 small onion, quartered	2 eggs
	1/4 cup white vinegar

1. Cut tripe into strips and wash in cold water.

2. Place tripe in a stockpot with water to cover. Add onion, celery stalk and 1/2 teaspoon salt and cook slowly for approximately 40-45 minutes or until tender.

3. Beat eggs in a bowl, using a fork. Add vinegar, 1 tablespoon water and a pinch of salt and beat again.

4. Add 1 cup of hot broth, 1/2 cup at a time, to the egg mixture, beating constantly. Then pour the egg/broth mixture back into stockpot and stir. Remove from heat and continue stirring for a minute or two. Season with salt and pepper. Serve at once. Tripe soup may be reheated very gently over low heat, stirring constantly. Do not bring to boil.

Cauliflower Soup

From Society Hill *Serves 6-8*

Make sure you "sweat" the onions, celery and carrots until very soft. This will give your soup a more concentrated flavor.

2 tablespoons butter

1 onion, chopped

1 celery rib, chopped

1 carrot, peeled and chopped

2 tablespoons chopped parsley

3 tablespoons chopped basil

1/2 head cauliflower, coarsely chopped

5-6 large mushrooms, sliced

1 quart chicken stock

Salt and pepper to taste

1. In a large saucepan, melt the butter, add the onions, celery, and carrots. Sauté until soft, about 10-15 minutes.

2. Add the remaining ingredients and simmer for about 1 hour. Season with salt and pepper to taste. Serve very hot.

Gazpacho

From Society Hill   **Spanish**   *Serves 10-12*

This is a very refreshing summer soup. The Tabasco gives a slightly hot flavor, so add more or less to taste.

1 large onion, chopped

1 large or 2 medium cucumbers, seeded and chopped

1 large green pepper, seeded and chopped

2 28-ounce cans Italian tomatoes

2 10 1/2-ounce cans beef consomme

1 1/2 cups V-8 juice

1/2 cup lemon juice

1/2 cup olive oil

2-3 hearty dashes Tabasco

2-3 teaspoons salt

1/4 cup fresh parsley, chopped

2 garlic cloves, crushed

1/2 teaspoon tarragon

1/4 teaspoon each of basil, marjoram, thyme, oregano and black pepper

1. Combine all the above ingredients together.

2. In a blender or food processor, process until desired consistency is reached. Do not blend too smooth; a slightly chunky consistency is more attractive. Chill well.

Serving suggestion: Serve with croutons or diced cucumber sprinkled on top.

Quick Cream of Broccoli Soup

From Fox Chase   *Serves 8*

This is a wonderfully light and tasty cream soup. Make it in large batches, as it freezes beautifully.

8 cups chicken broth (preferably homemade) (page 38)

2 cups broccoli stems (scrape off tough outer layer, and cut into 1-inch pieces)

1 medium onion, finely chopped

1/4 pound butter or margarine

1/2 cup flour

1 cup half-and-half

Salt and pepper to taste

1. In a food processor (or by hand) chop broccoli pieces very finely. Do not purée.

2. Bring chicken broth to a boil and add processed broccoli. Lower heat and simmer for about 15 minutes.

3. Meanwhile, in a saucepan, melt the butter or margarine and sauté the onion until transparent. When onion is tender, blend in flour on low heat and cook 1 minute, stirring constantly. Add the half-and-half and stir continuously until thoroughly blended. Add about a cup of hot broth to the flour/cream mixture and stir until thoroughly blended. Add this back slowly to the simmering broth. Continue to stir soup until completely blended.

4. Simmer slowly for 15 minutes. Serve.

Serving suggestion: After filling soup bowls, top with 1 table-spoon of finely chopped broccoli florets.

Variation: This basic cream soup can be varied by substituting the following vegetables for the broccoli: 1 cup of shredded rutabaga, 2 cups of coarsely chopped cabbage, 1 cup of shredded carrots, 2 cups of finely chopped celery, or 1 cup of fresh pumpkin. To prepare pumpkin for soup, peel and cube pumpkin and boil in water until tender. Drain and mash coarsely. This soup can also be made with any vegetable of your choice.

Lentil Soup

From Fox Chase   *Serves 8-10*

Lentils are available in red, yellow or brown. They are used in many traditional Easter dishes and year-round in hearty soups like this one.

1 pound brown lentils, cleaned
   and rinsed
2 1/2 quarts water
1/2 cup olive oil
1/2 cup chopped onion
1 cup chopped celery

1/2 cup chopped carrots
2-3 cloves garlic
Salt and pepper to taste
Red wine vinegar (optional)

1. Cover the lentils with water and bring to a boil. Reduce heat to low, cover and simmer for about 40-45 minutes.

2. Add the rest of the ingredients except for the vinegar. Simmer until vegetables and lentils are tender, about 30 minutes.

3. To serve, add a teaspoon of wine vinegar to each serving or bowl of soup. The wine vinegar is optional, but it enhances the flavor of the soup even more. If soup becomes too thick, simply add a little hot water.

Variation: Cook lentils with 2 ham hocks. When soup is done, remove meat from bones, chop and add to the soup. Eliminate olive oil from recipe. Also soup may be cooked with chicken or beef stock instead of water.

Bean Soup

From Queen Village   *Serves 6-8*

Dried beans are nutritious and filling and are wonderful and tasty in many soups. Lima or navy beans cooked with ham hocks are a good combination.

1/2 pound lima beans or navy beans, soaked overnight

2-3 ham bones or ham hocks

6 cups water

2 medium onions, chopped

3 carrots, diced

2 celery stalks, chopped

1 8-ounce can crushed tomatoes

1 teaspoon marjoram

1 teaspoon thyme

3 teaspoons pot herbs or soup greens

2 potatoes, diced

12-16 German dumplings (page 167)

1. Drain the soaked beans and reserve.

2. Place the ham bones or ham hocks in a stockpot and cover with about 6 cups of water. Bring to a boil, skim residue from surface, lower heat to medium and cook for 10 minutes, skimming occasionally.

3. Add the dried beans, onions, carrots, celery and canned tomatoes. Bring to a boil and simmer for 1 hour.

4. Meanwhile, prepare the dumplings.

5. After 1 hour, remove ham bones from soup, cut meat off the bone and shred. Put meat back into the soup. Add the rest of the herbs, potatoes and dumplings to the pot and simmer for about 45 minutes more. Soup can be made ahead of time and just heated through.

Serving suggestion: Serve with good crusty bread.

Lima Bean Soup

From Roxborough

Serves 4

This rich soup is more like a stew in consistency.

1 pound lima beans, soaked
   overnight, then drained

4-5 slices of thick bacon, diced

1/4 pound smoked ham, diced

1 onion, chopped

1 celery stalk, chopped

1 carrot, chopped

1 ham hock

2 cups chicken stock

2 cups water

Chopped parsley (garnish)

1. Fry the bacon until lightly browned, place on paper towel to drain.

2. In a large saucepan or stockpot, add all the ingredients including the bacon. Bring to a boil, then simmer for about 1 1/2-2 hours or until the beans are tender.

3. Remove the ham hock, sprinkle with parsley and serve.

Gourmet Bean Soup

From Germantown   *Serves 6*

This is a very tasty and nourishing soup for a cold winter's evening. Gourmet soup beans are a mixture of dried beans such as lentils, navy beans, black-eyed peas, lima beans and kidney beans.

1 pound gourmet beans,*
  soaked overnight

2 10-1/4 ounce cans tomato
  soup

2 medium onions, diced

2 celery stalks, diced

1 tablespoon lemon juice

Salt and pepper to taste

1 teaspoon thyme

2 cups water

1 smoked neck bone or ham
  hock (optional)

1. Drain the beans and put them into a large 3-quart stockpot. Add the rest of the ingredients and the neck bone or ham hock, if desired. (Adding a ham hock gives the soup a saltier flavor.)

2. Cover the pot, bring to a boil, then simmer for about 1 1/2 hours, or until the beans are tender.

Serving suggestion: Serve with a good crusty bread.*

*Available at specialty food shops.

Salads

Cucumber Salad

From Fishtown   *Serves 4*

A crisp and tasty salad. During the summer use the kerby cucumbers.

4 cucumbers, peeled, seeded
   and sliced

1 red onion, chopped

1 tablespoon red wine vinegar

Mayonnaise (homemade
   mayonnaise, page 214)

2 tablespoons sour cream

Salt and pepper to taste

1. In a bowl, mix all ingredients together. (Add enough mayonnaise to just coat the cucumbers.)

Serving suggestion: Serve with any broiled meat or fowl.

Variation: Add chopped red and/or green bell peppers for color.

Oriental Ginger Cucumbers

From Chinatown   **Chinese**   *Serves 6-8*

This salad is very refreshing to the palate and enhances any meal. To store fresh ginger, place in a jar or container, cover with vodka or dry vermouth and refrigerate. It will stay fresh for several weeks.

3-4 unwaxed cucumbers, sliced
1 tablespoon salt

MARINADE
3-4 slices fresh ginger, slivered
1/2 cup white vinegar
1/4 cup sugar
1/2 cup water
1 tablespoon sesame oil

Toasted sesame seeds (garnish)

1. Salt cucumbers and allow to sit for 1 hour. Rinse thoroughly under cold water and pat dry. Place in a bowl and reserve.

2. In a small saucepan, heat together the ginger, vinegar, sugar, water and oil. Bring to a boil, then pour over cucumbers. Marinate at least overnight.

3. To serve, garnish with toasted sesame seeds.

Variation: For a spicier flavor, add 1/2-1 teaspoon of hot chili flakes to the marinade.

Warmer Kartoffelsalat
Warm Potato Salad

From Olney **German** *Serves 4*

A nice change from the traditional cold potato salad. Serving the potato salad at room temperature brings out the flavor. Make sure to add the vinaigrette to the potatoes while they are still warm.

5-6 potatoes, boiled in their skins
1 small onion, finely chopped
3 tablespoons oil

2 tablespoons vinegar
1/2 teaspoon mustard
Salt and pepper to taste

1. Peel the potatoes as soon as possible after cooking. Slice potatoes and place in a salad bowl.

2. While the potatoes are still warm, add the chopped onions.

3. Whisk together the oil, vinegar, mustard, salt and pepper and pour over the still warm salad. Mix very gently so as not to break up the potatoes. Let the salad stand for a while; serve at room temperature.

Serving suggestion: This would be an excellent accompaniment to Wiener Schnitzel (page 130).

Old-Fashioned Dutch Potato Salad

From Manayunk   *Serves 8*

The red and green bell peppers add a splash of color to this traditional favorite.

5 large potatoes (about 2 1/2 pounds), boiled with skins on

Homemade mayonnaise (page 214)

1 tablespoon white vinegar, more or less to taste

1 red pepper, diced

1 green pepper, diced

1 stalk celery with leaves, diced

2 teaspoons celery seed

Salt and pepper to taste

1. When potatoes have boiled, cool and remove the skins. Cut into 1-inch cubes.

2. In a large bowl, spoon in 4 heaping tablespoons of mayonnaise (homemade or commercial). Add 1 tablespoon of white vinegar and whisk together.

3. Add the cubed potatoes, red and green peppers and celery seed. Little by little, add as much mayonnaise as you like. Season with salt and pepper to taste and refrigerate to cool.

Variation: Add 2 chopped hard-boiled eggs and/or 1 small chopped onion to potato salad.

Tabbouleh
Bulghur Wheat Salad

From West Philadelphia   **Syrian**   *Serves 4-5*

When bulghur (hulled wheat) is steamed until partially cooked, then dried and ground, it has a nutlike flavor. The fresh lemon juice adds a wonderful tangy flavor to the salad.

1 cup bulghur*

4 green onions, finely chopped, including green part

1 1/2 cups finely chopped Italian parsley

1/4 cup finely chopped fresh mint leaves

2/3 cup olive oil

1/2 cup fresh lemon juice

Salt and pepper to taste

Romaine lettuce leaves, washed and thoroughly dried (garnish)

---

1. Cover bulghur with cold water and allow to stand for 1-1 1/2 hours. Pour into a cheesecloth and squeeze out excess water. Allow to air-dry on a plate or cloth.

2. Add remaining ingredients, except lettuce leaves, and toss thoroughly. This is best done with your hands, squeezing the onions to release their juice into the salad.

3. Place tabbouleh on a platter and surround with lettuce leaves. The leaf lettuce is often used to scoop the tabbouleh.

Variation: Add 2 finely chopped cucumbers and 1 tomato, seeded and finely chopped, to the salad just before tossing and serving.

*Available at Middle Eastern and specialty food shops.

Israeli Salad

From the Northeast   *Serves 10-12*

This is an especially good and colorful salad to make for large gatherings.

2 green peppers, seeded

2 tomatoes

2 cucumbers

10 radishes

1 small head of white cabbage

1 small head of red cabbage

1 small head of iceberg lettuce

DRESSING

1/2 cup olive oil

1/3 cup fresh lemon juice

Salt and pepper to taste

1. Chop all the vegetables very finely and toss together in a large bowl.

2. Make dressing by whisking the lemon juice into the oil in a slow, steady stream until smooth and creamy.

3. Add dressing to salad just before serving. Season to taste.

Peking Summer Noodles

From Chinatown   **Chinese**   *Serves 8-10*

This spectacular dish is highly recommended for buffets or as picnic fare.

2 pounds fresh egg noodles
2 tablespoons sesame oil

SAUCE
2 tablespoons soy sauce
1/2 teaspoon Szechuan brown peppercorns*, heated and finely ground
2 tablespoons sesame paste*
1 tablespoon sesame oil
1/2 cup chicken stock
1/4 teaspoon hot chili pepper flakes (optional)
1 tablespoon rice wine vinegar

1/2 cup peanuts, toasted and chopped (garnish)

1. In a large pot, bring water to a boil. Drop noodles into water and cook for 3 minutes. Drain and rinse with cold water. Drain well again. Add the sesame oil to the noodles and arrange on a large platter.

2. In a bowl, mix together all the sauce ingredients. Blend well.

3. Pour sauce over the noodles and sprinkle with chopped toasted peanuts. Serve at room temperature.

*Available at Oriental and specialty food shops.

Thai Salad with Shrimp and Pork

From University City **Thai** **Serves 4**

Rice wine vinegar has a delicate flavor and is slightly milder than Western vinegars. If grape wine vinegar is substituted, reduce the amount used.

1 small head of lettuce, shredded
1 carrot, peeled and thinly sliced
1 red onion, sliced
1 tablespoon sugar
3 tablespoons rice wine vinegar
Pinch of salt

1 tablespoon water
1 teaspoon chili powder
8 shrimp, cooked, peeled and cut in half lengthwise
1/4 cup cooked pork, thinly sliced
1 hard-boiled egg, sliced

1. Soak all the vegetables in cold water for 15 minutes. Drain.

2. In a small saucepan, add the sugar, vinegar, salt and cook until syrupy. Add the water and chili powder. Stir well. Cool mixture.

3. In a salad bowl, combine the vegetables, shrimp and pork. Add the vinegar mixture, toss well and top with the sliced hard-boiled egg.

Maurie's Famous McDowell Colony Garlic and Blue Cheese Dressing

From Schuylkill   **Irish**   *Makes 1-2 cups*

This dressing is perfect for lovers of garlic and cheese.

1/4 cup lemon juice
1/2 cup oil
8 garlic cloves, minced
2-3 tablespoons Dijon mustard
  or any favorite mustard
1/4 cup blue cheese, crumbled

1. Place all the ingredients in a jar with a tight-fitting lid.

2. Shake very well and use over your favorite salad.

Serving suggestion: This goes especially well with a mixed arugula, spinach and watercress salad.

Meat and Fowl

Steak a la Savoyarde

From Head House Square   **Dutch**   *Serves 4*

This is an uncomplicated yet elegant dish. Using wines and spirits in cooking not only adds flavor, but also helps tenderize.

4 club or New York strip steaks
Salt and pepperg
Flour for dusting steaks
6 tablespoons sweet butter
1/2 pound Gruyere cheese,
   grated

SAVOYARDE SAUCE
1 tablespoon Madeira
1 tablespoon brandy
1 tablespoon port
1 cup heavy cream
Salt and pepper to taste
24 small mushrooms, cleaned,
   trim the stem ends

1. Prepare Savoyarde sauce. In a small saucepan, heat the Madeira, brandy and port; stir until thickened or syrupy. Add the heavy cream, stir and reduce to about a third. Sprinkle in salt and pepper to taste. Do not add mushrooms at this time. Reserve sauce.

2. Sprinkle the steaks with salt and pepper and lightly dust with flour. Heat the butter in a skillet. When hot, add the steaks and sauté 3-5 minutes on each side, or to desired doneness.

3. Place the steaks on a broiler pan, cover lightly with some of the sauce and sprinkle with Gruyere cheese. Broil just until the cheese has melted and is nicely browned.

4. Add the mushrooms to the reserved sauce and heat through. Place steaks on serving plates and pour on the sauce, distributing the mushrooms evenly. Serve at once.

Serving suggestion: Serve with a salad of assorted greens.

Sumpoog Yev Mees
Eggplant and Meat Casserole

From Center City   **Armenian**   *Serves 4*

The eggplant slices may be sprinkled with salt, placed on paper towels and patted dry after 30 minutes, if desired. This process can remove the bitterness of some eggplants.

1 pound ground beef or lamb or a mixture of both

1 medium eggplant, peeled and sliced into 1/4-inch rounds

Garlic salt and black pepper to taste

1 green pepper, coarsely chopped

1 onion, coarsely chopped

1 14-ounce can Italian plum tomatoes

1/2 cup tomato purée (optional)

1/2 cup water

Pinch of hot red pepper

1. Preheat oven to 325°.

2. Mix the meat with garlic salt and pepper. Add green peppers and onion and shape the meat mixture into patties. (Reserve any peppers and onions that do not hold together in the patties.)

3. In a casserole, place upright one eggplant slice, then a meat patty, then an eggplant slice. Repeat until full. Sprinkle with any reserved pepper or onions.

4. Pour over top the tomatoes, the purée (if used) and the water. Add a pinch of hot red pepper and cook uncovered for at least 1 hour or until eggplant is tender.

Serving suggestion: Eggplant and meat casserole goes well with pilaf, a green salad and hearty bread.

Smoked Tongue Supreme

From Spring Garden   *Serves 6*

*Tongue cooked this way is very tender and it tastes and looks
like baked ham. It will convince even the most squeamish to try
this variety meat.*

1 smoked beef tongue
  (3-4 pounds)

1 bouquet garni (made up of
  parsley, bay leaf and rosemary
  tied together)

1 leek, cleaned and sliced

1 onion, stuck with a clove

1 clove garlic, left whole

1 carrot, left whole

4 white peppercorns

2 tablespoons butter

1 small onion, chopped

2 celery stalks, chopped

2 eggs, lightly beaten

1 1/2 cups fresh bread crumbs

1 6-ounce can of tomato paste
  mixed with 1 cup port for
  basting

1. Soak the tongue overnight in cold water. Drain.

2. In a Dutch oven or casserole, place the tongue and cover
   with cold water. Add the bouquet garni, leek, onion with
   clove, garlic, carrot and peppercorns. Bring to a boil, then
   simmer for 3 hours or until the tongue is tender. Let cool
   in the broth.

3. Preheat oven to 350°.

4. Remove tongue from broth and pull off the skin, trimming
   the fat from the root of the tongue. Place in a roasting pan.

5. Melt the butter in a skillet. Sauté the onion and celery until
   soft, about 5 minutes. Allow to cool. Add the beaten eggs
   and bread crumbs to the onions; stir well to combine.

6. Mound the onion mixture over the top of the tongue. Bake
   for 30-40 minutes, basting occasionally with the tomato
   paste and port mixture. Slice and serve with the pan juices.

Ground Meat Pie

From University City   ***Serves 6***

The turmeric which adds color to foods also imparts a pleasant, pungent aroma to this dish.

2 pounds ground beef

1 slice white bread, soaked in 1/2 cup milk and mashed

2 tablespoons vegetable oil

2 onions, chopped

2 tablespoons curry powder

1 teaspoon turmeric

2 tablespoons lemon juice or rice wine vinegar

2 eggs

Pinch of salt

1/2 cup water

3-4 bay leaves

Almonds, chopped

1. Preheat oven to 350°.

2. In a skillet, heat the oil and fry the onions until soft. Add the mashed bread, curry powder, turmeric, lemon juice, and ground meat to the onions; mix thoroughly. Then stir in 1 well-beaten egg.

3. Grease an 8-inch pie dish and pour in the meat mixture. Bake for 1/2 hour.

4. After baking remove from the oven. Mix together the remaining egg, salt and water and pour over the ground meat. Place the bay leaves on top and sprinkle with a few chopped almonds. Return to the oven and bake for a further 1/2 hour.

Serving suggestion: Plain white rice or simply cooked vegetables such as broccoli, zucchini or snow peas would go well with this slightly spicy dish.

Meat in a Meal Dish

From South Philadelphia   **Italian**   *Serves 4-6*

The name of this dish is quite appropriate. It is truly a meal by it-self. The mashed potato crust, which is quick and easy to make, also helps to absorb the delicious filling.

1 pound sweet Italian sausage, casing removed

4-5 potatoes, peeled, cooked and mashed

1 large bunch of Swiss chard, washed, boiled, drained and chopped

4 eggs, beaten

4 ounces mozzarella, cut into cubes

1/4 cup grated Parmesan cheese

1. Preheat oven to 375°.

2. In a skillet, crumble the sausage meat and fry until browned.

3. In a 10-inch pie dish, mold the mashed potatoes to form a crust.

4. In a bowl, mix together the Swiss chard, browned sausage meat, mozzarella, beaten eggs and Parmesan cheese. Pour this mixture into the potato crust.

5. Bake in oven until the mixture is set, about 20-25 minutes.

Variation: Serve with a plain green salad with Maurie's garlic and blue cheese dressing (page 68).

Kalbsleber mit Wein
Calves Liver in Red Wine Sauce

From Olney   **German**   ***Serves 4***

Cloves, which are the dried flower buds of an evergreen tree, delightfully flavor the sauce for this dish. Cloves are used frequently in cooking to remove strong or unwanted flavors.

1 pound calves liver, thinly sliced	1/4 cup beef stock
3 tablespoons butter	1 bay leaf
1 small onion, halved, studded with 4-5 cloves	1 cup red wine

1. In a skillet, melt the butter and quickly sauté the liver for 1-2 minutes. Try not to overcook the liver as it becomes tough. Remove with a slotted spoon.

2. Add the onion halves, beef stock, bay leaf and red wine to the skillet. Let simmer for about 10 minutes or until the sauce has reduced by half and is slightly thickened.

3. Remove the onions and bay leaf.

4. Add the cooked liver to the sauce and very quickly heat through.

Serving suggestion: Rice would go well with this savory main dish.

Sauerbraten

From Olney   **German**   *Serves 6*

The long marinating and cooking process produces a superb flavor and mouth-watering tenderness.

3-4 pounds of beef round

MARINADE
2 1/2 cups red wine vinegar
1-2 cups water
2 bay leaves
2 cloves
1 teaspoon thyme

2 onions, chopped
1 carrot, diced

Oil for browning
1 cup beef stock
Salt and pepper to taste
Sour cream (optional)

---

1. In a saucepan, combine the marinade ingredients: vinegar, water, bay leaves, cloves, thyme, onions and carrots. Bring to a boil. Reduce heat, then simmer for 15 minutes. Allow to cool.

2. Place the meat in a non-metalic pan and pour in the cooled marinade; it should almost cover the meat. Add more water if necessary. Refrigerate for 4 days, turning the meat over at least twice each day.

3. When ready to cook, remove the meat and pat dry. Strain the marinade and reserve.

4. In a casserole, add a little oil and brown the meat. Add the vegetables from the marinade and gently fry them with the meat for about 5 minutes. Then add the marinade and beef stock. Cover the casserole with a lid and simmer on low heat for about 2 hours or bake in a 325° oven for about the same time or until the meat is tender.

5. Remove meat from the casserole and keep warm. Reduce the liquid slightly if necessary. A little sour cream may be added to the sauce, if desired.

Serving suggestion: German dumplings (page 167) would go very nicely with this tasty dish.

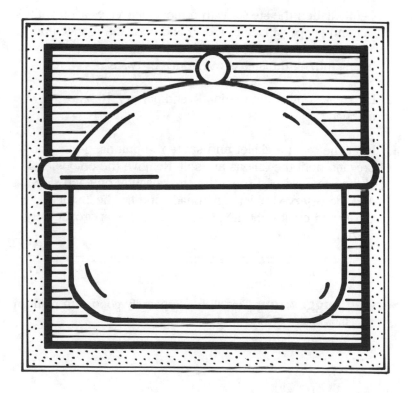

Bistec en Cazuela
Casseroled Beefsteak

From Fairhill   **Puerto Rican**   *Serves 6*

The orange and lemon juice gives this dish a special flavor.

6 small steaks
Salt and pepper
1/4 cup orange juice
1/4 cup lemon juice
4 tablespoons vegetable oil

5 onions, chopped
2 garlic cloves, chopped
1/2 teaspoon oregano
1/4 cup beef stock

1. Gently flatten the steaks with a meat cleaver. Season with salt and pepper. Place in a dish and pour the orange and lemon juice on top. Cover and refrigerate for about 3-4 hours, turning the steaks over once or twice.

2. Lift steaks out of the marinade and pat dry. Reserve the marinade.

3. Heat the oil in a skillet and sauté the onions, garlic and oregano until the onions are soft. Remove the onions and in the same skillet, brown the steaks lightly on each side. Add the reserved onions, marinade and the beef stock. Cover and cook until the steaks are tender, approximately 15-20 minutes.

Serving suggestion: This dish is especially good with plantain chips (page 179).

Carne Guisada
Beef Stew

From Logan **Puerto Rican** ***Serves 4***

Sofrito is a key ingredient in many Hispanic foods, and adds a certain spiciness to many of its dishes.

1 pound beef chuck, cut into cubes

1 tablespoon sofrito* (homemade, page 221)

1/4 pound smoked ham, cubed

1/2 cup green olives, pitted

1 8-ounce can tomato sauce

1 tablespoon brandy

1/4 cup water

1. Preheat oven to 350°.

2. In a large saucepan or casserole dish, place all the above ingredients together. Stir to mix.

3. Bring to a boil, then bake for 1-1 1/2 hours or until the meat is tender. During cooking, add more liquid if needed.

Serving suggestion: Noodles would make an excellent accompaniment.

*Available in Hispanic food stores.

Kalbi Gtui
Barbecued Beef Short Ribs

From Germantown   **Korean**   *Serves 4*

Beef, a popular meat in Korea, is wonderfully seasoned in this recipe with garlic, soy sauce and ground sesame seed.

2 1/2-3 pound beef short ribs, cut into 2-inch pieces

SEASONING SAUCE
6 tablespoons soy sauce

3 tablespoons sugar or honey

2 green onions, minced

1 large garlic clove, minced

2 tablespoons sesame seed* ground

2 tablespoons sesame oil

Black pepper to taste

2 tablespoons rice wine (optional)

1/2 pear

1. Trim excess fat from short ribs and pull off any tough outer skin.

2. With a sharp knife, score each piece diagonally in a 1/2-inch diamond pattern, leaving meat attached to the bone.

3. Combine all ingredients for seasoning sauce except for the pear.

4. Peel and grate the pear, adding its juice to the sauce.

5. Place the short ribs in the sauce and marinate for 1 hour.

6. Grill the ribs over charcoal or broil in the oven for approximately 20 minutes or until desired doneness.

Serving suggestion: Serve barbecued beef short ribs over steamed rice.

Variation: Take 1-2 green peppers, seeded and sliced, and 4 green onions, cleaned, trimmed, and cut into 2-inch pieces and cook alongside the shortribs.

*Available at Oriental and specialty food shops.

Stir-Fry Sliced Beef

From West Philadelphia　　　**Thai**　　　*Serves 6-8*

To make the beef easier to slice paper-thin, freeze it slightly before slicing.

2 pounds beef (flank steak or London broil), thinly sliced

3 tablespoons soy sauce

1 tablespoon minced ginger

1 tablespoon light brown sugar

1 tablespoon rice wine vinegar

3 tablespoons vegetable oil

2 scallions, chopped

1. In a bowl, combine the beef, soy sauce, ginger, brown sugar, vinegar and 1 tablespoon of oil. Marinate for 2-3 hours.

2. In a wok or skillet, heat 2 tablespoons oil until hot. Add the drained beef (reserving the marinade), and stir-fry for 1-2 minutes or until pink just disappears. Add remaining marinade and cook for 30 seconds more. Sprinkle with scallions.

Serving suggestion: This dish can be served over rice or noodles or by itself at room temperature.

Philadelphia Corned Beef

From Queen Village   **Jewish**   *Serves 6-8*

Corned beef surrounded by a variety of vegetables is a wonderful winter warmer. Equally wonderful are the sandwiches and hash made from the leftovers.

1-1 1/2 pounds fresh corned beef
Water

1. Wash corned beef thoroughly in cold water to remove excess brine.

2. Fill a stockpot with water and bring to a boil. Place the meat in the water; cover and bring to a simmer. Cook for approximately 1 1/2 hours or until meat is fork-tender.

3. Remove from heat; uncover and allow meat to cool in the broth to prevent shrinkage.

4. When cooled, remove from broth and slice against the grain.

Serving suggestion: Corned beef is excellent with old-fashioned Dutch potato salad (page 63), or your favorite potato or cabbage recipe and ice-cold beer.

Heart-Shaped Meat Loaf

From Queen Village   *Serves 4*

A romantic twist for an everyday-type meal. Equally good hot or cold.

1 3/4 pounds ground beef

2 eggs

1/4 cup milk

1 large green bell pepper, diced

1 medium onion, diced

1 cup dry bread crumbs

1 tablespoon chopped fresh parsley

Salt and pepper to taste

1. Preheat oven to 350°.

2. In a blender or food processor, add eggs, milk, green pepper and onion; purée well.

3. In a bowl, put the ground beef, bread crumbs, parsley, salt and pepper. Pour in the egg mixture and mix thoroughly by hand.

4. Place the meat mixture into a heart-shaped mold or form a heart shape on a baking sheet. (If you prefer, use a regular loaf pan.)

5. Bake meat loaf for 1 hour.

Serving suggestion: Serve meat loaf with mushroom gravy (page 217) or basic tomato sauce (page 220).

Pastelón
Plantain and Meat Casserole

From Olney   **Puerto Rican**   *Serves 4*

Plantains are similar to bananas but have dark brown skins and are used mainly for cooking. In this dish, interestingly enough, they add a cheese-like flavor.

1 pound ground beef

1 tablespoon adobo sauce*

1 teaspoon sazon seasoning*
  or 1 teaspoon garlic powder
  and 1 teaspoon onion powder,
  mixed

1 8-ounce can tomato sauce

2-3 plantains

Oil for frying plantains

Butter for greasing the pan

2 eggs

1. In a bowl, mix the ground meat, adobo and sazon seasonings together.

2. In a skillet, add the meat mixture and brown. Pour in the tomato sauce and simmer for 1/2 hour.

3. Meanwhile peel the plantains and cut lengthwise into 3 slices. In a skillet, add a little oil and very gently fry the plantains. Use a very low heat as they tend to crisp quickly and not cook through enough. The plantains should be very soft and light golden in color.

4. Preheat oven to 350°.

5. Butter a lasagna pan. Place a layer of the plaintains on the bottom, then a layer of meat, and repeat.

6. Beat the eggs and pour over the top layer. Bake in the oven for 45 minutes or until the egg has set.

Serving suggestion: Rice is a natural complement to this dish.

*Available in Hispanic food stores.

Chicken Satay

From University City　　　　**Thai**　　　　*Serves 4*

One of the ingredients used in this recipe is tamarind, a dark brown fruit shaped like a broad bean with a half-moon curl. To extract the juice, soak a piece in warm water until soft, then strain through a fine sieve.

2 pounds of boneless chicken breasts cut into l-inch strips

MARINADE

1 tablespoon oil

3 tablespoons light cream

1/2 cup coconut milk

3 slices ginger, crushed

3 cloves garlic, crushed

1 tablespoon curry powder

1 tablespoon powdered coriander

1 teaspoon salt

PEANUT BUTTER CURRY SAUCE

1 1/2 cups coconut milk or light cream

1 tablespoon red curry paste*

1 tablespoon roasted chili curry paste*

2 tablespoons peanut butter

1 tablespoon sugar

1 tablespoon lemon juice or tamarind* juice

Wooden skewers, soaked in water

Salt to taste

1.　In a bowl, place the chicken strips together with the marinade mixture, toss gently and let marinate for at least 2 hours.

2.　Prepare peanut butter curry sauce. Heat the coconut milk until boiling. Add the two kinds of curry paste and cook for a few seconds. Add the peanut butter, sugar, salt and lemon or tamarind juice. (Tamarind usually comes in a semisoft block. Break 1 or 2 pieces off and place in warm water for 2-3 hours. Strain to obtain juice.) The sauce should have a salty, sweet and sour taste. Serve as a dipping sauce for the chicken.

3. Thread a few pieces of the chicken strips onto the wooden skewers. Cook over charcoal or broil for about 5 minutes. While cooking, baste with a little coconut milk.

Serving suggestion: A cool cucumber salad would be very refreshing served with or after the satay.

*Available at Oriental and specialty food shops.

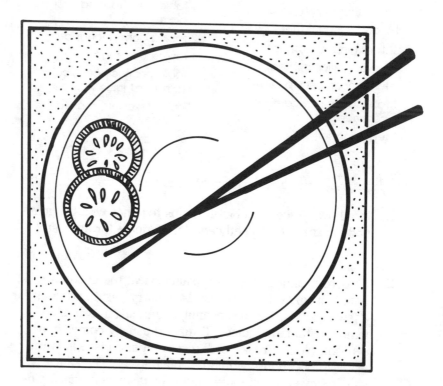

Gallina en Pepitoria
Chicken in Almond Sauce

From North Philadelphia   **Puerto Rican**   ***Serves 8-10***

Cinnamon stick, cloves and almonds give this dish its haunting flavor.

6 whole chicken breasts, halved, skin removed

Flour for dredging

3 tablespoons olive oil

2 onions, finely chopped

3 garlic cloves, minced

1 large tomato, peeled, seeded and chopped

1/3 cup chopped parsley

1 2-inch cinnamon stick

4 whole cloves

2 cups chicken stock

2 tablespoons almonds, blanched and finely ground

Salt and pepper to taste

3 teaspoons lime juice

2 eggs

1. Dredge the chicken pieces in flour; shake to remove excess flour.

2. In a skillet, heat the oil and sauté the chicken pieces until golden
in color. Transfer to a casserole or Dutch oven. In the same skillet, sauté the onion and garlic until soft. Add the tomato, parsley, cinnamon stick, cloves, chicken stock and almonds. Season to taste. Then pour sauce into the casserole. Cover and simmer for 30-35 minutes or until the chicken is tender.

3. Remove chicken pieces from the casserole and keep warm. Reduce the sauce by half over high heat. Strain the sauce through a fine sieve into a smaller saucepan. Place on low heat.

4. Meanwhile beat the eggs with the lime juice and whisk in a little of the heated sauce. Then pour this slowly back into the sauce. Let simmer for a few minutes to thicken, then pour over the chicken. Do not let the sauce boil or it will curdle.

Serving suggestion: Serve with plain rice or noodles and green beans sautéed in butter.

Chicken and Gravy

From Whitman   *Serves 4*

An old-fashioned dish but popular as ever.

8-10 chicken thighs

3 tablespoons vegetable oil

1 large onion, chopped

8-10 tablespoons flour

3-4 tablespoons soy sauce or A1 sauce

1/4 pound mushrooms, wiped clean and sliced

Salt and pepper to taste

1. Heat oil in a skillet and sauté the onions until lightly colored. Add the chicken thighs and cook, turning once or twice for 5-10 minutes.

2. Gradually add the flour, sprinkling it over the chicken and mixing it thoroughly with the oil. Cook chicken with flour for 5-10 minutes, turning the pieces occasionally. The flour should be thoroughly incorporated.

3. Add enough hot water to come halfway up the sides of the chicken and simmer uncovered for about 1-1 1/2 hours, or until chicken is tender and sauce reduced.

4. Add the mushrooms and soy sauce and cook for another 5-10 minutes.

Serving suggestion: Serve over rice or with mashed potatoes or biscuits and a green vegetable.

Sweet and Sour Chicken

From Society Hill   *Serves 4*

This is a no-fuss chicken dish with a marvelous taste. The unusual combination of ingredients produces a delicious sweet and sour sauce.

1 whole chicken, cut into parts
Poultry seasoning
1 cup apricot preserves
1 packet onion soup mix
1/4 cup lemon or orange juice

4 tablespoons Worcestershire sauce
Pineapple slices and cherries (optional)

1. Preheat oven to 350°.

2. Season chicken pieces with poultry seasoning and place in a baking pan. Bake for 40-50 minutes.

3. Meanwhile in a bowl, mix together the apricot preserves, onion soup mix, fruit juice and Worcestershire sauce.

4. When the chicken has cooked for approximately 40 minutes, pour the sauce over the chicken and cook another 20-30 minutes, or until chicken is done. Run briefly under the broiler to crisp. Garnish with pineapple slices and cherries, if desired.

Serving suggestion: This dish is quite good served with rice and a green salad.

Dajaj Meshwi bi Toum
Chicken with Garlic

From Bella Vista   **Lebanese**   *Serves 4*

Garlic has been used since ancient times for its medicinal value and is an essential ingredient in this recipe.

1 whole chicken, cut into parts
1 tablespoon white vinegar
Water
2 tablespoons butter

1 whole bulb of garlic, peeled
  and mashed
2 tablespoons lemon juice
Salt and black pepper to taste

1. Place the chicken pieces in a large bowl and sprinkle with salt. Add the vinegar and cover with water. Marinate for 1-2 hours. Drain and pat dry. This method helps to tenderize the chicken. (Use this method for other chicken dishes.)

2. In a skillet, melt the butter and brown the chicken pieces. Reduce the heat; add the mashed garlic and saute gently for a further 1-2 minutes. Add the lemon juice and enough water to come halfway up the sides of the chicken.

3. Bring to a boil, reduce heat to medium and cover. Cook for 10 minutes. Uncover and continue cooking for about 1 hour, or until the chicken is cooked through and the juices have reduced.

Serving suggestion: Serve with plain rice and use pita bread to dip into the sauce.

Sate
Skewered Grilled Chicken

From Head House Square   **Indonesian**   *Serves 4*

It is interesting to compare this Indonesian sate with the Thai satay on page 98. The Indonesian version uses soy sauce as a main ingredient. The Thai sauce favors curry flavorings.

1 pound of chicken breasts, skinned and boned

1 small onion, minced

2 garlic cloves, minced

2 teaspoons sugar

1/2 teaspoon salt

1 tablespoon olive oil

1 1/2 teaspoons soy sauce

Juice of 1 lemon

8 small skewers, soaked in water

PEANUT BUTTER SAUCE

1 tablespoon vegetable oil

1 small onion or 2 shallots, minced

1 garlic clove, minced

2 tablespoons peanut butter

1 tablespoon soy sauce

1 cup milk

1. Cut the chicken into small cubes. In a bowl, combine the onion, garlic, sugar, salt, oil, soy sauce and lemon juice. Mix thoroughly. Add the chicken cubes, toss and allow to marinate for 1/2 hour or longer.

2. Prepare the peanut butter sauce. In a small saucepan, heat the oil. Add the onion and garlic and sauté gently for 5 minutes. Add the peanut butter and soy sauce and mix well. Pour in the milk, stirring constantly, and cook the sauce until smooth and creamy, about 20-25 minutes. If sauce becomes too thick, add a little more milk.

3. Put the chicken pieces on the skewers and grill for about 5 minutes on each side. These may also be cooked in the broiler for the same amount of time.

4. Serve with the peanut butter sauce.

Serving suggestion: Sate can be served over rice as a main dish. As an appetizer chicken pieces can be served with cocktail toothpicks and the sauce as a dip.

Conejo Tapado
Smothered Rabbit

From Mount Airy **Puerto Rican** *Serves 4*

Rabbit is becoming more readily available in food markets. However, this dish may also be made with chicken. When cooking rabbit or chicken pieces, it is possible that the legs may need a little more time.

1 rabbit, about 2 pounds, cut into pieces

4 garlic cloves, finely chopped

1 onion, finely chopped

3 tomatoes, peeled, seeded and chopped

1 tablespoon olive oil

2 tablespoons capers

1/4 cup dry sherry

1 teaspoon oregano

Salt and pepper

8-10 new potatoes, scrubbed

12 pimiento-stuffed olives, halved

1. Preheat oven to 350°.

2. Place the rabbit pieces into a large casserole or Dutch oven. Cover the rabbit with the chopped garlic and onions, together with the tomatoes, oil, capers, sherry, oregano, salt and pepper.

3. Cover and bake for 30-35 minutes. Add the potatoes and cook for a further 30 minutes or until the potatoes and rabbit are cooked. Just before serving, add the olives.

Serving Suggestion: Serve with a plain green salad or sautéed green beans or asparagus in season.

Philadelphia Fried Chicken

From Queen Village   *Serves 4*

This could be the best fried chicken you will ever have. In this recipe flouring the chicken and refrigerating for 1 hour will produce a crispy, crusty chicken.

1 whole chicken cut into pieces   1 cup milk
Flour for coating chicken   Salt and pepper to taste
3 eggs   Oil for frying

1. Place the flour on one plate. Mix the eggs and milk together in a bowl.

2. Dip chicken pieces into the flour, then into the egg mixture and coat once more with flour. Place in one layer on a plate and refrigerate 1 hour.

3. Using if possible a black cast-iron skillet, fill with oil about 3/4 of the way up the pan. When the oil is hot (test by sprinkling a little flour in the oil and if it splatters, the oil is ready), add the chicken pieces, a few at a time. Cover, slightly reduce heat if necessary, and cook for 15-20 minutes or until chicken is done, turning once or twice during the cooking process. Drain on paper towels and serve.

Serving suggestion: Serve with old-fashioned Dutch potato salad (page 63) or coleslaw and biscuits.

Chicken Wellington with Stilton

From Olde City   *Serves 6*

Stilton is an English cheese traditionally served at the end of a meal with port. In this dish the cheese complements the chicken with great style. It can be assembled several hours ahead of time and baked when needed.

6 chicken breasts, boned and skinned

Double recipe of cream cheese pastry (page 259)

4 tablespoons butter

2 tablespoons vegetable oil

1/2 pound Stilton cheese

2 tablespoons sour cream

Salt and pepper

1 egg beaten for glaze

---

1. In a skillet, melt the butter and oil, gently fry the chicken until lightly browned, about 2-3 minutes.

2. Divide the pastry into six pieces. Roll each piece large enough to cover the chicken breasts.

3. In a bowl, mash together the Stilton and sour cream.

4. Preheat chicken to 350°.

5. Place a chicken breast on top of the pastry, spread a little of the Stilton on top, and wrap the pastry around the chicken to form an envelope shape. Place seam side down on a baking tray and brush with egg glaze. Repeat with the remaining chicken pieces.

6. Bake in oven for 35-40 minutes, or until the pastry is lightly browned.

Serving suggestion: A mixed green salad with mustard dressing would go well with this dish.

Pheasant in Madeira Sauce

From Fitler Square   *Serves 4*

Braising in the Madeira sauce will give the pheasant a moist tenderness.

2 pheasants, 2 1/2-3 pounds
  each, skinned and halved

6 tablespoons butter

1 tablespoon oil

1 onion, finely chopped

1 cup Madeira

1/2 cup chicken stock

2 large celery root, peeled and
  sliced medium thick

Salt and pepper

1. Preheat oven to 375°.

2. In a skillet, melt the oil and butter. Sauté the pheasant halves on each side about 2-3 minutes. Remove to a roasting pan or large casserole dish.

3. In same skillet, sauté the onions until soft and add to the roasting pan. Pour over the Madeira and stock. Cover and bake for 30 minutes.

4. Meanwhile, in the skillet, add a little more butter if necessary and gently fry the celery root on both sides until lightly browned. When pheasant has cooked for 30 minutes, add the browned celery root to the casserole and cook for a further 10-12 minutes or until the celery root is tender.

5. Remove pheasant and celery root to a platter and keep warm. Reduce the liquid by half. Season with salt and pepper and pour over the pheasant. Serve.

Arroz con Pollo
Chicken with Rice

From Kensington   **Puerto Rican**   *Serves 4*

Sofrito and sazon are used in many Hispanic dishes, and they give this chicken and rice recipe a zesty flavor.

1 whole chicken, cut into pieces

2 tablespoons oil

2 tablespoons sofrito* (page 221)

1 8-ounce can tomato sauce

1 package of sazon* or
  1 teaspoon of garlic powder
  and 1 teaspoon of onion
  powder, mixed

2 cups rice, uncooked

1 cup chicken stock

1 cup water

2 tablespoons coriander,
  chopped (optional)

1. In a skillet, heat the oil and brown the chicken pieces on all sides. Add the sofrito, tomato sauce and sazon, simmer for 2-3 minutes.

2. Distribute the rice around the chicken and add the chicken stock and water. Cover the pan and simmer until the rice is cooked, about 45 minutes. Sprinkle with coriander.

Serving suggestion: Serve with a mixed green salad or sautéed green beans.

Variation: Add frozen peas toward the end of the cooking.

*Available at Hispanic and specialty food shops.

Chicken Romano

From Roxborough   *Serves 4*

This quick and easy dish is excellent for dinner parties. It is colorful, attractive and very tasty.

4 chicken breasts, boned and skinned

4 tablespoons butter

1/2 cup pimientos, diced

1/4 cup black olives, pitted and sliced

1/2 cup mushrooms, sliced

1 cup heavy cream

1 cup grated Romano cheese

---

1. Melt the butter in a skillet and sauté the chicken until done. (Be careful not to overcook.) Remove chicken from skillet.

2. Add the pimientos, olives, mushrooms, cream and cheese. Simmer gently until the sauce has reduced and thickened. Remove from heat and serve over the chicken.

Serving suggestion: Serve with rice and green beans or broccoli.

Mediterranean Chicken

From Art Museum Area   *Serves 10*

This most colorful version of baked chicken is perfect for a large gathering.

10 whole chicken breasts, skinned, boned and halved

3/4 cup all-purpose flour

Salt and pepper

3 tablespoons butter

3 tablespoons olive oil

1 teaspoon oregano

1 large garlic clove, minced

2 cups dry red wine

1 12-ounce can frozen orange juice concentrate, thawed

10 large mushrooms, sliced thinly

2 large red onions, sliced into rings

2 large green peppers, sliced into rings

1 cup Greek olives, chopped

1. Combine flour, salt and pepper. Dust chicken lightly in mixture.

2. Heat 2 tablespoons each of butter and oil in a large skillet over medium heat. Stir in oregano and garlic. Add chicken in batches and sauté until golden brown on both sides. Add more butter and oil to skillet, if necessary. Transfer chicken to a large casserole or Dutch oven and set aside. Reserve skillet in which chicken was cooked.

3. Preheat oven to 375°.

4. Combine wine and orange juice concentrate in a bowl and blend well. Add to the skillet in which chicken was sautéed and cook uncovered about 2-3 minutes, scraping bottom of pan. Pour sauce over chicken breasts. Cover and bake 30 minutes.

5. Heat 1 tablespoon butter and 1 tablespoon oil in same skillet in which chicken was browned. Add mushrooms, onions

and green pepper and sauté over medium heat until slightly softened, about 3-4 minutes. Reserve.

6. After the chicken has baked for 30 minutes, spoon mushroom, onion, and green pepper mixture over chicken. Top with chopped olives and bake uncovered for an additional 30 minutes, basting every 10 minutes until chicken is tender and well glazed.

Serving suggestion: Plenty of crusty bread is a satisfying accompaniment for the richly flavored sauce of this delightful Mediterranean dish.

Roast Chicken with Lemon

From Fox Chase   *Serves 4*

Simple to prepare and the best roast chicken ever. It makes a perfect Sunday dinner.

1 whole chicken, about 2-1/2
  pounds
Juice of 1/2 lemon

Salt and pepper to taste
3 tablespoons butter, melted

1. Preheat oven to 350°.

2. Wash the chicken thoroughly with cold water, inside and out. Pat dry with paper towels, inside and out.

3. Place in a roasting pan and rub lemon juice all over chicken. Season with salt and pepper.

4. Roast for approximately 20 minutes, then pour melted butter on top. Continue cooking another 60-70 minutes or until done, basting chicken periodically with drippings. A little water should be added to pan to prevent drippings from burning during cooking.

5. Remove chicken from oven and allow to rest for 5-10 minutes before carving. Chicken broth can be used for basting and also to make a gravy for the roast chicken.

Serving Suggestion: Serve with Zucchini Parmigiano (page 174) or bulghur pilaf (page 199). It also goes well with vegetables and any favorite potato dish.

Roast Loin of Pork with Sauerkraut and Dumplings

From Queen Village   **German**   *Serves 6-8*

An incredibly delicious and juicy way of preparing pork.

1 loin of pork, 5-5 1/2 pounds
(have the butcher chine the
bone for easy carving)

1 large onion, quartered

1/2 teaspoon marjoram

1/2 teaspoon thyme

1/2 teaspoon sage

Salt and pepper to taste

Sauerkraut and dumplings
(page 167)

---

1. Preheat oven to 350°.

2. Place loin of pork in roasting pan. Place quartered onion on top of pork loin and secure with toothpicks.

3. Season pork loin with marjoram, thyme, sage, salt and pepper. Place in oven and roast uncovered for 1 hour, then remove onions from top of roast and continue roasting another 1-1 1/2 hours or until done. (If using a meat thermometer, it should register 170°-175°.)

4. Meanwhile, cook sauerkraut and dumplings and reserve.

5. Remove roast from oven and allow to rest 10-15 minutes before carving. (This resting period will allow meat juices to settle and roast will be much juicier.)

6. Reheat sauerkraut and dumplings and serve alongside.

Carne de Porco a Alentiejana
Pork and Clam Casserole

From Olney   **Portuguese**   *Serves 4*

The pork and clam combination in this recipe is a beautiful blending of flavors enhanced with the sprinkling of coriander. A truly unique experience in dining.

1 pound lean boneless pork, cubed

1-2 garlic cloves, minced

1/2 cup white wine

Salt

1 teaspoon Tabasco, more or less to taste

2 medium potatoes, diced

Vegetable oil for frying potatoes and pork

2 dozen littleneck clams, scrubbed clean and well-rinsed

1/3 cup black olives, pitted and chopped

Coriander (also called cilantro), chopped

1. Marinate the pork cubes in the garlic, white wine, salt, and Tabasco for several hours or overnight.

2. Cover the bottom of a 12-inch skillet with vegetable oil and fry the diced potatoes until cooked and slightly browned, about 20 minutes. Reserve.

3. Lift pork cubes from marinade, reserve marinade. In a skillet, heat 2 tablespoons of oil and fry the marinated pork cubes until browned. Add the reserved marinade and clams to skillet. Cover and cook over medium heat about 10-15 minutes, or until clams open. Discard any clams that do not open.

4. Add the fried potatoes to the clams and pork. Then add the black olives and coriander. Serve at once.

Baked Pork and Sauerkraut

From Fox Chase   **Hungarian**   *Serves 4*

Kümmel seeds are used in many Hungarian pork dishes, especially goulash. If unavailable, use caraway seeds.

1 pork roast, 3 1/2-4 pounds,
  boned, rolled and tied

Garlic powder

Salt and pepper to taste

1 28-ounce can sauerkraut

Kümmel seeds (optional)

1. Preheat oven to 350°.

2. Place the pork in a baking pan and sprinkle with garlic powder, salt and pepper to taste. Bake in the oven, uncovered, approximately 1-1 1/4 hours.

3. Remove from oven and add the sauerkraut around the roast. Add 3/4 cup of water and sprinkle with kümmel seeds, if desired. Return to oven and bake for another 45-60 minutes, or until pork is cooked through. (If using a meat thermometer, it should register 170°.) Remove pork and sauerkraut from pan. Let pork roast rest 5-10 minutes before slicing. (This allows the juices to settle into the meat and the roast will be juicier.) Serve sliced with sauerkraut.

Serving suggestion: Baked pork with sauerkraut goes well with mashed potatoes and mushroom gravy (page 217).

Plommonspackad Flaskkarre
Pork Loin with Prunes

From the Swedish Museum,   **Swedish**   *Serves 4*
Packer Park

Prunes are perfect with pork. They add color, texture and a wonderful flavor to the pork fillets.

2 pork tenderloin filets (about 1 1/2 pounds each)

6-8 dried pitted prunes, soaked in warm water for 1 hour

2 teaspoons salt

1/8 teaspoon white pepper

1/4 teaspoon ground ginger

3 tablespoons vegetable oil

2 cups chicken stock

1. Drain the prunes, keeping a little of the liquid in reserve.

2. Place 1 pork fillet on table and lay the prunes close together down the center. Cover with the second piece of pork. Press together and tie at intervals with string. Rub the pork all over with the salt, pepper and ginger.

3. Preheat oven to 350°.

4. In a large casserole or Dutch oven, add the oil and brown the pork on both sides on the stove. Add the stock and bake in the oven for 35-40 minutes. Add more stock or a little of the reserved prune juice toward the end.

5. Take out the pork and let rest. Meanwhile, reduce the juices over medium heat and serve with the pork. Slice the pork and serve with reduced juices.

Variation: Try this dish with red cabbage (page 165).

"Toad in the Hole"
Sausage Puffs

From Center City   **British**   ***Serves 6-8***

This can be enjoyed for dinner or for a special breakfast treat.

1 pound small breakfast sausages
or large sausages cut into
1-inch pieces

1 cup flour

Pinch of salt

2 eggs

1 cup milk

3 tablespoons shortening or oil

---

1. Preheat oven to 400°.

2. In a bowl, sift the flour and salt. Add the eggs and milk a little at a time. Beat until the batter is smooth. This can be done in a food processor or blender.

3. Poach the sausages in a saucepan with water to cover for about 5 minutes.

4. Place the shortening or oil in a baking pan and put into the oven until very hot, but not smoking or burning. Pour in a layer of batter, place the sausages on top and cover with another layer of batter. Return to the hot oven and bake for about 30 minutes. The pudding should puff up slightly.

Serving suggestion: Serve with a tossed green salad.

Variation: Spicy sausage, such as Italian hot or sweet or chorizo, can also be used for this dish

Tamal en Cazuela
Ham and Cornmeal Casserole

From Chestnut Hill   **Cuban**   *Serves 4*

This recipe duplicates the flavor of tamal, which is made with freshly ground corn, but it has been adapted over the years so that you can find the ingredients easily.

1 tablespoon olive oil

1 medium onion, finely chopped

1 green pepper, finely chopped

1 8-ounce can tomato sauce

1/4 pound ham, diced

1 3/4 cups yellow cornmeal

1/4 cup water

1 8 1/2-ounce can creamed corn, lightly mashed in a blender or food processor

1 5-ounce can evaporated milk

1 tablespoon red wine

Salt and garlic powder to taste

1. In a skillet, heat the oil and add the onions and peppers. Fry for 1-2 minutes, then pour in the tomato sauce and add the ham. Cook over low heat for 2-3 minutes.

2. In a large saucepan, pour in the cornmeal, moisten with water and then add the creamed corn and evaporated milk. Start cooking this mixture over low heat. When it is hot, add the onion and green pepper mixture (called sofrito), together with red wine. Season with salt and garlic powder.

3. Cook the "tamal" over low heat, stirring occasionally to prevent sticking, for about 45 minutes to an hour. Serve hot.

Serving suggestion: A mixed green salad or plain white rice would go well with this dish.

Pork Chop Casserole

From Fishtown   *Serves 8*

An easy, uncomplicated pork chop casserole for those busy days. This dish is a favorite with children.

8 pork chops, 1/2-inch thick

1-pound package of egg noodles, cooked and drained

1 tablespoon butter

1-2 onions, chopped

1 14-ounce bottle of tomato ketchup

1/2 tablespoon Worcestershire sauce

1 cup bread crumbs

1. Preheat oven to 350°.

2. Add 1 tablespoon of butter to the cooked noodles and toss.

3. Place 4 pork chops in a casserole large enough to hold them comfortably. Cover the chops with half the onions and half the noodles. Add another layer of chops, onions and noodles. Pour the ketchup over the noodles and add Worcestershire sauce; then sprinkle bread crumbs over the top. Bake in the oven for 1 hour.

Serving suggestion: This dish is good with corn or peas sprinkled with fresh mint.

Kielbasa with Red Cabbage and Apples

From Port Richmond　　　　**Polish**　　　　*Serves 4*

This is a good, tasty winter dish. Kielbasa comes fresh or smoked. In this recipe either can be used.

2 pounds kielbasa sausage

2 tablespoons vegetable oil

1 tablespoon butter

2 small onions, finely chopped

1 small head red cabbage, shredded

2-3 Rome apples, peeled, cored and sliced (1/4-inch thick)

2 bay leaves

1/4 cup red wine vinegar

1/2 cup beef stock

Salt and pepper to taste

1. In a casserole or Dutch oven, heat the oil and butter, and sauté the onions until soft.

2. Add the cabbage and apples and mix well. Place the kielbasa and bay leaves into the cabbage and toss gently to mix. Add the vinegar, salt and pepper. Cover and simmer for approximately 40 minutes.

3. Remove the bay leaves and kielbasa.

4. Transfer the cabbage to a serving platter and arrange the kielbasa on top. Serve.

Serving suggestion: Serve with some crusty bread and butter.

Carne de Puerco en Chili Verde
Pork in Creamy Pepper Sauce

From The Parkway   **Mexican**   *Serves 6*

This dish can be made more fiery by adding extra chili peppers to taste. When using fresh chilies, remember to wash your hands well afterwards.

1½-2 pounds of boneless pork roast or pork fillets

3 tablespoons oil

Salt and pepper

3 cups white wine or chicken stock, or a combination of both

2 cloves garlic, unpeeled

1 onion, peeled

2 green pepper, halved

2 fresh chilies (canned chilies may be substituted)

1/2 cup sour cream

3 tablespoons coriander (cilantro), chopped

Sprigs of coriander (garnish)

1. In a heavy casserole or Dutch oven, brown the meat in the oil. Sprinkle with salt and pepper, then pour in the wine and/or chicken stock. Cover and let simmer for 1-1 1/2 hours.

2. Meanwhile, coat the garlic, onion, green peppers and green chili pepper with oil, place on a baking sheet and bake at 375° for 10-15 minutes. Remove from the oven and cool. When cooled, peel the garlic and quarter the onion. Peel as much skin as you can from the green peppers and chili peppers, and remove the seeds and stalks. Put all this into a blender or food processor, together with the sour cream and coriander. Purée until smooth.

3. In a skillet, cook the puréed sauce for about 5 minutes, or until slightly thickened.

4. When pork is cooked, remove from casserole and keep warm. Reduce remaining liquid from the casserole until syrupy. Pour this into the pepper purée mixture. Taste for seasoning. Add a little salt and pepper, if necessary.

5. Cut pork into fairly thick slices and place them in the sauce. Let simmer very gently for about 5 minutes, until the meat heats through.

Serving suggestion: Plain rice is the perfect accompaniment to this slightly spicy dish.

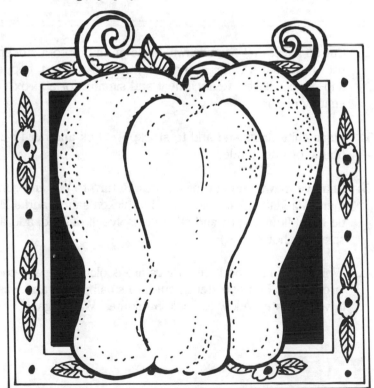

Hog Maws and Chitterlings
with Collard Greens

From South Philadelphia   **Soul Food**   *Serves 4-6*

This dish is basic to soul cooking. A pot of mixed greens is usually served alongside.

HOG MAWS AND CHITTERLINGS
1 pound hog maws
 (pig stomach)
1 pound chitterlings
 (hog intestines, also called
 chitlins)
1 1/2 quarts water
1/2 teaspoon salt

1/2 teaspoon pepper
Red pepper flakes to taste
Hot sauce (optional)

COLLARD GREENS
1 bunch collard greens
1 ham hock, split
Water

1. Cut off excess fat from maws. Rinse and put into a stockpot with 1 1/2 quarts water. Bring to a boil and add salt, pepper and pepper flakes. Reduce heat and simmer for approximately 1 hour.

2. Rinse chitterlings and add to stockpot. Cook another 1 1/2 hours, or until tender.

3. Remove maws and cut into pieces. Return to pot and simmer an additional 45 minutes. (To thicken sauce, add a little bit of flour to pot and stir to dissolve. If desired, add a splash of hot sauce.)

4. While hog maws and chitterlings are cooking, prepare collard greens. Remove stems, cut into small pieces and wash in warm water. Allow to soak 15 minutes. Wash again.

5. Place ham hock in water to cover and bring to a boil. Reduce heat and cook slowly for about 1 hour.

6. Add washed greens to pot and cook about 50 minutes, or until tender.

Serving suggestion: This flavorful combination is made even better with a side dish of cornmeal bacon dumplings (page 198).

Gratin of Potatoes, Ham, Eggs, and Onions

From Andorra   *Serves 4*

A very tasty gratin. Imported, top-quality ham should be used.

2 tablespoons vegetable oil

4 tablespoons butter

1 small onion, finely chopped

1/4 cup diced ham

4 eggs

1 garlic clove, crushed

2 tablespoons chopped parsley,
   chives or chervil

1/2 cup grated Swiss cheese

4 tablespoons milk or light cream

Pinch of salt and pepper

2 medium potatoes, peeled
   and shredded

---

1. Preheat oven to 350°.

2. In a skillet, heat the oil and 1 tablespoon of butter. Add onions and cook slowly until softened, but not browned.

3. Raise the heat slightly, stir in the ham and cook for a few seconds longer.

4. In a bowl, beat together the eggs, garlic, herbs, cheese, milk or cream, salt and pepper. Pour this into the ham mixture.

5. Squeeze out any excess water from the potatoes and stir into the egg mixture.

6. Add 1 tablespoon of butter to an 11 × 12-inch baking dish or individual baking dishes about 6 inches in diameter. Heat to melt the butter. Pour in the potato and ham mixture, dot with the remaining butter and bake for about 30-40 minutes, or until the top is nicely browned. Serve directly from the pan.

Serving suggestion: This is very tasty as an individual dish, but it also goes well with roast chicken.

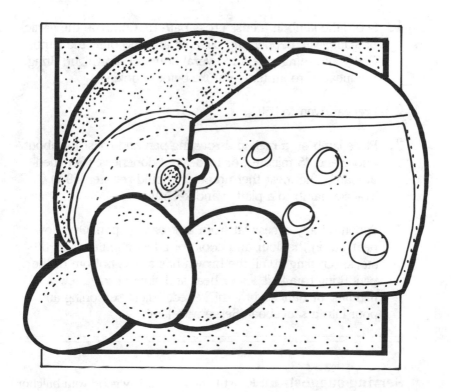

Roast Leg of Lamb

From Overbrook   *Serves 4*

For a more pronounced garlic flavor, make several l-inch-deep slits in the lamb and insert garlic slivers prior to cooking. This is a very aromatic way of cooking lamb.

1 leg of lamb, 2 1/2-3 pounds
  (shank portion)

2 cloves garlic, minced

2 teaspoons oregano

Salt and pepper to taste

1/4 cup olive oil

1 tablespoon flour

1 cup chicken stock

1. Score the lamb in a criss-cross pattern. Combine the garlic, oregano, salt, pepper and olive oil and rub onto the lamb. Cover and refrigerate for several hours or overnight. Bring the meat to room temperature before cooking.

2. Preheat oven to 350°.

3. Place lamb on a rack in a roasting pan and roast for about l hour and 45 minutes, or to desired doneness. (For medium lamb, the meat thermometer should register l60°.) Transfer lamb to a platter and keep warm.

4. Spoon off any excess fat from the roasting pan. Over low heat, stir in the flour and cook for a few minutes. Add the stock, scraping up all the brown bits at the bottom of the pan. Bring to a boil, lower heat and simmer for a few minutes, or until slightly thickened. Adjust seasoning and pour into a sauceboat. Serve with lamb.

Serving suggestion: Roast lamb is especialy good with bulghur pilaf (page 199) and a green vegetable.

Riñones con Jerez
Kidneys with Sherry

From North Philadelphia   **Puerto Rican**   *Serves 4*

A nicely flavored dish for variety meat fanciers. Kidneys require a brief cooking process to avoid further toughening.

8 lamb kidneys
1 tablespoon butter
1 tablespoon vegetable oil
1 onion, finely chopped

Salt and pepper
6 tablespoons dry sherry

1. Remove skin and any fat from the kidneys. Slice lengthwise and soak in water for about 20 minutes. (This will remove any bitter taste from the kidneys.) Drain and dry well.

2. Heat the butter and oil in a skillet and sauté the onions until soft and lightly browned. Remove with a slotted spoon and reserve.

3. Add a little more butter, if necessary, to the skillet and sauté the kidneys for about 5 minutes. Do not overcook. Return onions to the skillet, add the sherry and cook for 1-2 minutes more.

Serving suggestion: This dish is delicious by itself, served over rice or on buttered toast.

Variation: Use 1 pound of veal kidneys, thinly sliced, and cooked as above.

Mashbat ad-Darwish
Stewed Lamb with Vegetables

From Bella Vista   **Lebanese**   *Serves 4*

In Lebanon, as in many of the Middle Eastern countries, lamb is a traditional favorite. This presentation of lamb is made using a few simple ingredients with wonderful results.

1 pound lamb, cut into cubes

3 tablespoons butter

1-2 large garlic cloves, minced

1 onion, chopped

2 small potatoes, quartered

1 small can tomato paste or 1/2 cup tomato sauce

1/2 cup water

Salt and pepper to taste

1. In a large skillet, melt the butter and sauté the lamb until browned on all sides. Remove lamb.

2. In the same skillet, add the garlic and onions and cook 1-2 minutes. Add the sautéed lamb, potatoes, tomato paste or sauce, water, salt and pepper to taste. Cook uncovered for about 1 hour or until the lamb and potatoes are done. During the last half hour of cooking, add more water to sauce, if necessary, and cover pan with lid slightly askew.

Serving suggestion: Serve with pita bread to dip in sauce.

Variation: Try adding different vegetables to the stew, such as okra, eggplant and beans (dried or fresh).

Lamb Stuffed with Oysters

From Head House Square　　　　　　　　　　***Serves 6***

The use of oysters in cooking dates back to Colonial times. Even the shells of the oysters were used to pave streets.

1 leg of lamb (shank), boned and butterflied

1 cup bread crumbs

2 hard-boiled eggs, chopped, yolks only

4 anchovies, chopped

1 small onion, chopped

1 teaspoon rosemary

1 teaspoon summer savory

1/8 teaspoon mace

12-14 oysters, chopped

2 eggs, beaten

Salt and pepper

BURGUNDY SAUCE

3/4 cup clam juice

1/2 cup Burgundy

3 anchovies, chopped

Pinch of mace

1 tablespoon chopped onion

9 oysters, chopped

Pan juice from lamb

1. Preheat oven to 350°.

2. In a bowl, mix together the bread crumbs, egg yolks, anchovies, onion, rosemary, summer savory, mace and oysters.

3. Add the beaten eggs, enough to bind the mixture together. (Mixture shouldn't be too sticky.)

4. Place the butterflied lamb on the counter and spread the stuffing down the middle. Roll and tie firmly with string.

5. Roast in the oven, 30 minutes per pound, or to desired doneness.

6. Prepare Burgundy sauce. In a saucepan, combine all the ingredients except for the pan juices. Simmer for 5-8 minutes. Add the deglazed pan juices (deglaze by adding 1 tablespoon of water to the pan). Heat the sauce through and serve with the lamb.

Agnello con Salsa Rosa e Olive Nere
Lamb with Red Sauce and Black Olives

From Girard Estates   **Italian**   *Serves 4*

This is sure to become one of your favorite lamb dishes. The combination of herbs produces a superb flavor.

1 pound of young lamb, cut in cubes

1/4 cup olive oil

1/2 teaspoon salt

1/4 teaspoon black pepper

1/3 teaspoon garlic powder

4 large sage leaves (1/4 teaspoon dried sage can be substituted)

1 teaspoon rosemary

3/4 cup white wine

1/2 cup Italian plum tomatoes (fresh or canned), chopped

1/2 cup black olives (preferably oil-cured), pitted

1. In a heavy 10-inch skillet, combine the oil, lamb cubes, salt, pepper, garlic powder, sage and rosemary. Cover and place on low heat, turning the lamb frequently until it is golden brown and starts sticking to the bottom of the pan. This takes between 45 and 60 minutes. (There is some juice in the pan at the start of cooking time, but it reduces and the lamb begins to brown.)

2. When the lamb has browned, add the wine, increase the heat and cook for about 5 minutes. Then add the tomatoes and olives, reduce heat and simmer until the lamb is tender.

Serving suggestion: This dish goes well with peas, spinach or boiled Italian greens.

Veal "Volcano Style"
Rolled Veal Tenders Filled with Mozzarella

From Rittenhouse Square   **Italian**   *Serves 4*

This is a wonderful veal dish, especially with the added surprise of cutting into it and finding a burst of melted cheese.

12 small veal tenders, pounded very thinly

8 slices white bread, processed to crumbs in blender or food processor

2 tablespoons chopped Italian parsley

1 clove garlic, minced

Salt and pepper to taste

1/4 cup olive oil

12 cubes of mozzarella

4 skewers

1. Combine bread crumbs, parsley, garlic, salt and pepper.

2. Dip each veal tender in olive oil and shake off excess. Then coat with the bread crumb mixture.

3. Place a cube of cheese in the center of each slice and roll. Continue with remaining tenders.

4. Place 3 rolls on each skewer. Arrange in a shallow pan and broil on the middle rack of the oven for 5-8 minutes or until golden brown on each side. Serve.

Serving suggestion: The skewered veal tenders can be served on a bed of rice along with a green vegetable such as asparagus or broccoli.

Veal Ossobuco

From Roxborough　　　　　**Italian**　　　　　***Serves 4***

This is a less complicated version of the traditional Northern Italian favorite. The veal is braised until fork-tender.

4 veal shanks

Flour

1/4 cup (4 tablespoons) butter

1 onion, chopped

2 garlic cloves, chopped

1 carrot, diced

1 celery stalk, diced

2 fresh tomatoes, peeled and chopped

1 cup beef broth

Salt and pepper

1.　Preheat oven to 350°.

2.　Dust veal shanks with flour.

3.　Melt butter in a casserole or Dutch oven large enough to hold the veal shanks comfortably. Brown the veal on both sides and remove.

4.　Add the onions, garlic, carrots and celery and sauté until they have wilted slightly. Add the tomatoes, reserved veal shanks and beef broth. Cover and bake in the oven for 1-1 1/2 hours. When cooked the meat should be very tender, almost falling off the bone. Check during cooking that the juices do not run dry; if so, add a little more beef stock or dry vermouth. If the juices are too thin at the end of cooking, remove the veal shanks, place the casserole on high heat and reduce until thickened.

Serving suggestion: This dish is good with crusty bread, rice mixed with Parmesan cheese, or noodles with sautéed green beans.

Wiener Schnitzel
Breaded Veal Cutlets

From Olney   **German**   *Serves 4*

A wonderfully flavored veal entrée using simple ingredients.

4 veal cutlets (each about 6 ounces), lightly pounded

Salt and pepper

Flour

1 egg, lightly beaten with 1 teaspoon water

1 cup plain bread crumbs

1/3 cup vegetable shortening

2 tablespoons butter

Lemon wedges (garnish)

1. Sprinkle cutlets lightly with salt and pepper. Dredge with flour. Dip into egg mixture, allowing excess egg to drip off. Then coat completely with bread crumbs, patting them lightly. Refrigerate for 1 hour. (This allows the crumbs to adhere better during frying.)

2. In a skillet large enough to hold the cutlets comfortably, heat the shortening and butter together. When hot but not smoking, add the cutlets and fry until golden brown on both sides.

3. Remove to a serving platter and garnish with lemon wedges.

Serving suggestion: Wiener schnitzel goes well with almost any vegetable side course. Try it with warm potato salad (page 62) or a tossed green salad with garlic and blue cheese dressing (page 68).

Gulyas
Goulash

From Northern Liberties   **Hungarian**   *Serves 6*

In this classic Hungarian dish, it is preferable to use Hungarian paprika. Because of the long, slow cooking, the goulash makes its own juices, so no other liquid should be needed.

1 1/2 pounds of veal or pork, cubed

3 tablespoons vegetable oil

3 onions, chopped

3-4 tablespoons paprika (preferably Hungarian sweet)

4-5 tomatoes, peeled, seeded and chopped

1/3 cup red wine vinegar

1/2 tablespoon kümmel seed (caraway or anise seed may be substituted)

Pinch of marjoram

Salt and pepper to taste

1. Heat the oil in a skillet and brown the meat evenly on all sides. Remove with a slotted spoon to a casserole. Add the onions to the skillet and gently sauté until well cooked, about 15-20 minutes. Transfer to the casserole with the meat. Add the paprika and cook, stirring to coat the meat and onions well for about 4-5 minutes.

2. Add the garlic, tomatoes, red wine vinegar, kümmel or caraway seeds and marjoram. Season with salt and pepper. Bring to a boil, then reduce heat and simmer covered for 1-1 1/2 hours, or until the meat is fork-tender.

Serving suggestion: Buttered noodles or German dumplings (page 167) go well with this dish.

Variation: To make goulash soup, add 1 28-ounce can of Italian plum tomatoes.

Fish and Shellfish

Psito Psari
Baked Whole Fish

From the Northeast   **Greek**   *Serves 4*

Oregano and rosemary are frequently used in Greek cooking. When using dried herbs, bruise them slightly by rubbing them with your fingers to release the flavor. This dish can also be prepared with fish fillets.

4 small fish (such as porgy, sea bass or red snapper), cleaned and with head left on)
Juice of 1 lemon
Salt and pepper to taste
2 tablespoons olive oil
1 teaspoon oregano
1 teaspoon rosemary
4 bay leaves

SAUCE
2/3 cup olive oil
1/2 cup fresh lemon juice, or to taste
Water

1. Preheat oven to 350°.

2. Make 2 or 3 slits in fish (1-inch long cut only into top half of fish). Rub with lemon juice and season with salt and pepper. Place in a pan that has been lightly greased with olive oil. Sprinkle with oregano and rosemary and place a bay leaf on top of each fish.

3. Bake in oven for approximately 40 minutes, or until fish is done. Run fish under the broiler for a minute or so to crisp the skin. Serve with oil/lemon sauce.

4. To make sauce, beat the lemon juice into the olive oil with a fork in a slow, steady stream. Add a little water and continue beating until smooth and creamy.

Serving suggestion: This dish goes very well with boiled greens such as endive or escarole or a tossed green salad.

Machi Pulao
Fish Curry with Rice

From University City   **Indian**   *Serves 4*

Curry is not a spice but a mixture known as garam masala. Garam means "hot" and masala *means "spice" and it is used in many Indian dishes.*

CURRY MIXTURE
1 tablespoon ground coriander
2 teaspoons ground cumin
1/2 teaspoon ground ginger
1 teaspoon turmeric
1/2 teaspoon chili powder
Water
1 1/2 tablespoons vegetable oil

FOR FISH
2 cups water
2 pounds white fish fillets
  (flounder, cod, fluke)
Salt to taste
1 1/2 tablespoons vegetable oil
2 onions, sliced
1 cup rice, uncooked
2 tablespoons fresh lemon juice

1. To prepare the curry: In a small bowl, combine coriander, cumin, ginger, turmeric and chili powder. Mix thoroughly. Add enough water to make a thick paste. Heat the oil in a large casserole and stir in the curry paste. Cook over medium heat until the spices darken, about 3 minutes.

2. Add 2 cups water to the casserole and bring to a boil. Then add the fish fillets. Season with salt to taste. Reduce heat and simmer until the fish flakes, about 10 minutes. With a slotted spoon, remove the fish fillets and keep warm. Reserve liquid.

3. Heat 1 1/2 tablespoons oil in a skillet and sauté the onions until translucent. Add the reserved fish liquid and bring to a boil. Stir in the rice and lemon juice. Cover the skillet and simmer the rice over low heat until cooked, about 20 minutes.

4. Add fish, warm through and serve.

Serving suggestion: Traditionally served with a green vegetable and Indian chappatis (page 278) and for dessert gulab jamun (page 225).

Samak Magli
Fried Fish

From Bella Vista   **Lebanese**   *Serves 4*

Orzo is a pasta similar to rice in shape. It adds color and a slight crunchiness to the rice. The contrast between the hot rice and fish served at room temperature gives this dish its interesting appeal.

4-5 fillets of white fish (flounder, haddock, cod)

2 tablespoons butter

2 tablespoons chopped walnuts

2 tablespoons pine nuts

1/2 cup orzo

1 cup uncooked rice

2 teaspoons allspice

3 cups water

1. Heat butter in a skillet. Fry the fish gently about 2-3 minutes on each side. Remove from pan and reserve.

2. In the same skillet, toast the nuts and remove. Reserve.

3. Using the same skillet, add a little more butter if necessary, brown the orzo, add the rice and stir until well coated with butter. Sprinkle with allspice and pour in 3 cups of water. Lower heat to a simmer, cover the skillet and cook for about 20 minutes or until the rice is cooked.

4. Spread the rice onto a large platter and place the fish fillets on top. Sprinkle with the toasted nuts and serve.

Layered Fish Casserole

From Society Hill   ***Serves 8-10***

A wonderful combination of flavors and textures. This is a lovely and delicious dish. It can also be assembled in advance and cooked just prior to serving.

6 pounds small flounder fillets

3/4 pound scallops

1/4 pound lump crab meat

2 pounds shrimp, peeled and deveined

1 dozen fresh oysters

Fresh bread crumbs

Salt and pepper

2 tablespoons dill, chopped

1 tablespoon parsley, chopped

1/3 cup lemon juice

4 tablespoons butter

Lemon slices

Paprika

1. Preheat oven to 350°.

2. Butter a large casserole.

3. On the bottom of the casserole, place half the flounder fillets, skin side down. Divide the scallops, crab, shrimp and oysters and place on top of the flounder.

4. Sprinkle with bread crumbs, salt, pepper, 1 tablespoon of dill, 1/2 tablespoon of parsley, half of the lemon juice and dot with 2 tablespoons of butter.

5. Repeat with one more layer. Bake for approximately 30 minutes.

Serving suggestion: Serve with a green salad with garlic and blue cheese dressing (page 168). Plain rice would also be a good accompaniment.

Baked Fish with Paprika

From Northern Liberties   **Hungarian**   *Serves 4*

This Hungarian favorite is both delicate and very tasty. If possible use real Hungarian paprika which has a sweet flavor. Regular paprika, which can be harsh or tasteless, is not recommended for this dish.

6 fish fillets (perch or flounder)

3 potatoes, peeled and cooked

Butter to grease baking dish

Salt and pepper

Paprika

1 green pepper, finely chopped

3 tomatoes, peeled, seeded and chopped

1 medium onion, minced

1/2 cup sour cream mixed with 1/2 cup plain yogurt or heavy cream

1. Preheat oven to 400°.

2. When potatoes have cooled, slice into medium-thick slices.

3. Butter the bottom of a casserole.

4. Layer the bottom with the sliced potatoes. Sprinkle with salt and pepper.

5. Place the fish fillets over the potatoes and sprinkle with salt, pepper and paprika.

6. Spread the chopped green pepper, tomato and onion over the fish.

7. Dollop the top with a mixture of sour cream and yogurt and sprinkle with a little more paprika.

8. Bake for 10 minutes then reduce to 350° and bake for 15-20 minutes longer. To brown the top, run under the broiler for 1-2 minutes. The fish bastes in its own juices during cooking.

Serving suggestion: Serve with a fresh green vegetable or a salad.

Shin Shu Mushi
Steamed Fish Filled with Noodles

From Washington Square West   **Japanese**   *Serves 4*

Mirin is a sweet rice wine and is used in cooking instead of sugar as it has a more mellow sweetness and adds a glaze to sauces. Sake is a rice wine used to add zest to cooking. It is also served warm in small porcelain cups during the meal.

1/2 pound matcha men*
(Japanese-style noodles)

4 pieces fillet of flounder or fluke (medium-size slices), sprinkled with a little salt

2 cups chicken broth

3 tablespoons sweet rice wine (Mirin)

2 tablespoons sake

2 tablespoons light-colored soy sauce

1 medium slice daikon, grated (with excess liquid removed) and sprinkled with cayenne pepper

---

1. Bring a pot of water to a boil. Add matcha men noodles and cook 4-5 minutes. Drain and rinse thoroughly in cold water. Drain again.

2. Take one slice of fish, place one-fourth of the noodles on top and roll. Secure with toothpicks. Repeat with the remaining fish fillets and noodles.

3. Put the rolls in a casserole and place in a pot of boiling water (water should come halfway up the dish). Cover pot and steam for about 10 minutes, or until fish just flakes with a fork.

4. In another saucepan, add chicken broth, rice wine, sake and soy sauce. Heat.

5. Place steamed fish rolls in 4 bowls, top with daikon/ cayenne pepper mixture and ladle hot chicken broth sauce over fish. Serve.

*Available at Oriental food stores.

Samak bi-Taratur
Spicy Fish

From Bella Vista　　　　**Lebanese**　　　　***Serves 4***

Wrapping brown paper or foil around fish is similar to steaming by sealing in the moisture and juices and is a delicious way of preparing fish. Tahini is a paste made from sesame seed and is used in many Middle Eastern recipes.

1 whole fish, 3-4 pounds (bass, trout, red snapper), cleaned and split open (fish fillets can be substituted)

1 lemon, cut into pieces

2 tomatoes, chopped

1/2 cup chopped parsley

2 tablespoons olive oil

3 tablespoons pine nuts, toasted

TAHINI SAUCE

1 cup tahini sauce*

1 garlic clove

2 tablespoons lemon juice

Dash of Tabasco

1/2 cup water

1. Preheat oven to 350°.

2. Take some brown paper or foil and cut a piece large enough to wrap around the fish.

3. Place half of the brown paper or foil on a baking tray and lay the fish on top. Place half of the cut-up lemon, tomatoes and parsley inside the fish. Sprinkle the rest over the top.

4. Dribble olive oil over the fish, then cover with the other half of the brown paper or foil. Pinch paper or foil together and bake 15-20 minutes or until done (cooking time will vary depending on thickness of fish). Remove fish from the paper and place on a platter. Sprinkle with toasted pine nuts and serve with tahini sauce.

5. To prepare sauce, mix all ingredients together in a food
processor or blender until smooth.

*Available at Middle Eastern and specialty food shops.

Dover Sole with Tarragon Wine Sauce

From Society Hill   **British**   *Serves 2*

This is a very traditional English dish that has stood the test of time. Tarragon has a delicate lemon and licorice flavor and complements the sole beautifully.

2 small whole Dover sole, gutted (retain roe if any)

Flour, seasoned with salt

4 large sprigs of tarragon

1 cup dry white wine

Black pepper

2 tablespoons butter

1. Preheat oven to 350°.

2. Roll the sole in the seasoned flour.

3. Melt the butter in a casserole and sauté the fish in the butter with a sprig of tarragon under each fish. Cook for 2 minutes.

4. Add the wine and the rest of the tarragon. Turn the heat down and reduce for 5 minutes. Then place in the oven for 10 minutes to reduce the liquid further. Remove tarragon and reserve the sauce.

5. Carefully remove the meat from the bones and pour some sauce over each portion. Season with pepper.

Serving suggestion: Serve with buttered spinach and mashed potatoes.

Flounder with Anchovy and Cheese Sauce

From Society Hill   **British**   *Serves 4*

This unusual combination of anchovy paste and Cheddar cheese enhances the delicate flavor of the flounder and makes this an outstanding dish.

4 flounder fillets
Salt and white pepper
1 tablespoon butter

WHITE SAUCE
2 tablespoons butter
2 tablespoons flour
1 1/2 cups milk
1 tablespoon anchovy paste
1 cup grated Cheddar cheese

1. Butter a casserole and lay flounder fillets on the bottom. Sprinkle with salt and white pepper. Dot pieces of butter onto each fillet.

2. Place under the broiler for about 8 minutes or until the fish flakes when tested with a fork. To avoid dryness do not overcook.

3. Prepare the white sauce. In a saucepan, melt the butter, then add the flour. Stir the flour and butter for a few seconds. Gradually add the milk and stir until smooth and thickened. Add the anchovy paste and Cheddar cheese. Mix well. Pour over the fish and run under the broiler for another 2 minutes.

Serving suggestion: Serve with boiled or mashed potatoes or peas with mint.

Fresh Tuna Bake

From South Philadelphia   Italian   *Serves 4*

Fresh tuna is well worth trying. It is meaty and slightly oily which also makes it an excellent fish for grilling. Prepared this way, it is very moist and succulent.

4 slices of tuna, 1-inch thick

1 onion, coarsely chopped

2 garlic cloves, minced

1 15-ounce can of tomatoes, drained

1 red sweet pepper, coarsely chopped

1 tablespoon parsley, chopped

1 tablespoon fresh basil, chopped

4 tablespoons olive oil

1 small box frozen peas

Salt and pepper to taste

1. Preheat oven to 350°.

2. In a bowl, mix onions, garlic, tomatoes, red pepper, parsley, and basil together.

3. In a skillet, heat the oil and sear the tuna on both sides.

5. Place in an oven-proof dish, pour all the chopped vegetables over the fish. Add the frozen peas, cover and bake for 10-15 minutes. To check for doneness, the fish should flake easily when pierced by a knife.

Serving suggestion: Any leftover tuna bake makes a wonderful sauce for pasta.

Baccala en Salsa
Codfish in Tomato Sauce

From South Philadelphia   **Italian**   *Serves 4*

When buying, look for baccala that is well dried and white in color, not yellowish. Some fish stores have baccala already pre-soaked.

1 1/2 pounds baccala (dried salted cod fish)	1 28-ounce can Italian plum tomatoes, drained
Flour	4 teaspoons capers
Olive oil for frying baccala plus 2 tablespoons for sauce	1/4 pound black oil-cured olives, pitted and chopped
2 garlic cloves, minced	

1. Soak baccala in a roasting pan, with cold water to cover, in the refrigerator for 2 days, changing water often. Thicker pieces may require longer soaking to remove saltiness.

2. Wipe baccala dry and cut into 3-inch square pieces. Coat with flour and fry in heated olive oil until browned.

3. To make sauce, heat 2 tablespoons olive oil in a saucepan. Add the minced garlic and sauté 1 minute. Add the plum tomatoes and cook approximately 15 minutes. Add capers and olives and cook another 5 minutes.

4. Preheat oven to 325°.

5. Place fried baccala in a baking dish. Pour sauce over top and cover. Bake in oven for approximately 20 minutes. Serve baccala with pan juices.

Serving suggestion: Rice and a mixed green salad go well with this dish.

Kalamari Yiahni
Stewed Squid with Olives and Red Wine

From the Northeast   **Greek**   *Serves 4-6*

Squid is tender, delicious and easy to cook. When buying fresh squid, look for a milky white appearance. The wine and olives give this dish a piquant flavor.

1 1/2-pounds small squid, cleaned (see page 151) and thoroughly rinsed

1/2 cup olive oil

1 medium onion, sliced

2 green bell peppers, seeded and sliced

1/2 cup chopped parsley

3 tablespoons tomato sauce

Salt and pepper to taste

1/3 cup dry red wine

1/3 cup green olives, pitted and halved

1. Cut squid sac into rings, 1-inch wide. Separate tentacles and cut in half if large.

2. Heat oil in a flame-proof casserole and sauté onion for 1-2 minutes until softened. Add squid and cook over medium-high heat for 10 minutes. (Squid will release its juices.)

3. Add green pepper, parsley, tomato sauce, salt and pepper to taste. Lower heat and simmer for approximtely 30 minutes or until squid is tender and easily pierced with a fork.

4. Add wine and olives and simmer an additonal 5-10 minutes.

Serving suggestion: Rice pilaf makes an excellent accompaniment.

Calamari e Piselli
Sautéed Squid and Peas

From South Philadelphia   **Italian**   *Serves 4-6*

Squid is best cooked quickly for 1-2 minutes or for a long period of time. Anything in between tends to toughen the squid.

3-4 pounds squid

1/4 cup olive oil

1 garlic clove, crushed

1 small onion, diced

2 cups tomatoes, chopped

1 bay leaf

1 teaspoon basil

Salt and pepper to taste

1 10-ounce bag frozen peas or 1 pound fresh peas, cooked

How to Clean Squid

Hold the sac with one hand and gently pull out the tentacles with the other. The insides of the sac should come away with the tentacles. Cut the tentacles above the eyes, remove the small bony beak, reserve the tentacles and discard everything else. Remove the quill-like bone from the sac and thoroughly wash the sac, inside and out, removing anything left inside. Peel the skin off the sac under running cold water. Rinse the sac and tentacles thoroughly, then dry and refrigerate until ready to cook.

1. Cut the prepared squid into 1-inch pieces, leaving the tentacles whole.

2. In a large saucepan, heat the oil. Sauté the garlic and onion in the oil until soft and translucent. Add the tomatoes, bay leaf, basil, salt and pepper.

3. Add the squid and simmer for 45 minutes.

4. Add the peas and cook for another 10 minutes, stirring frequently.

Serving suggestion: This dish is wonderful as a sauce over pasta or served in soup bowls with crusty bread for dipping.

Garides me Feta
Shrimp with Feta Casserole

From Rittenhouse Square   **Greek**   *Serves 4*

Feta is a sharp, salty white cheese that is still made mostly from goat's milk. Try to buy feta that has been soaking in brine. If you buy vacuum-packed feta, place in a bowl and cover with milk. This will keep it creamy and fresh longer.

1 1/2 pounds shrimp, shelled and deveined

Juice of half a lemon

1/3 cup olive oil

6 scallions, cleaned, trimmed and chopped

1 large garlic clove, minced

1 35-ounce can whole Italian plum tomatoes, along with some of the purée from the can

1/4 cup chopped fresh parsley

Pinch of sugar

Salt and pepper to taste

1/2 cup dry vermouth

4 tablespoons sweet butter

1 teaspoon oregano

1/2 pound feta, crumbled

1. Squeeze lemon juice on shrimp and reserve in refrigerator.

2. In a large skillet, sauté scallions in olive oil. Add garlic, tomatoes, parsley, pinch of sugar, salt and pepper. Simmer 20-25 minutes. (During cooking process, break tomatoes into pieces using the side of a spatula.) Add vermouth and simmer 10 minutes longer.

3. In another skillet, heat butter and sauté shrimp quickly until they just turn pink. Do not overcook. Add sautéed shrimp to the simmering tomato sauce. Sprinkle oregano and crumbled feta evenly over top. Cover pan and simmer just until feta has softened, approximately 5 minutes. Serve at once.

Serving suggestion: Shrimp with feta is wonderful served over rice or with crusty bread for dipping sauce.

Shrimp and Mushroom Casserole

From Chestnut Hill
Serves 4

This casserole is perfect for dinner parties. It can be assembled ahead and heated through prior to serving. Use medium or large shrimp.

1 1/2 pounds shrimp, shelled and deveined

4 tablespoons butter

1/2 pound mushrooms, cleaned and sliced

1/2 teaspoon salt

1 teaspoon oregano

1 teaspoon thyme

Freshly ground pepper to taste

4 large garlic cloves, mashed

2 tablespoons chopped fresh parsley

1. Preheat oven to 375°.

2. In a saucepan of water, blanch the shrimp for 1 minute. Drain.

3. In a skillet, melt the butter and sauté the mushrooms for 3-5 minutes. Add salt, oregano, thyme, pepper, garlic and parsley.

4. Add the drained shrimp and mix. Put into a baking dish and bake for 12 minutes.

Serving suggestion: Serve over pasta or rice, or put into patty shells.

Shrimp with Lemon Butter Sauce

From West Philadelphia *Serves 4*

This can also be served as a first course. The lemon and garlic add a Mediterranean flavor to this very delicious dish.

1 1/2 pounds shrimp, shelled, deveined and butterflied

8 tablespoons butter

1/4 cup fresh lemon juice

1 teaspoon garlic powder, or 2 large garlic cloves, minced

1/4 cup fresh parsley, chopped

4 green onions, chopped (garnish)

1. Melt the butter and add the lemon juice.

2. Place shrimp in a pan suitable for broiling and pour the lemon butter over the shrimp. Sprinkle with garlic and chopped parsley and run under the broiler for 5-7 minutes, until the shrimp are just done. Do not overcook.

3. Garnish with green onions and serve with pan juices.

Serving suggestion: Serve over fettucine or linguine.

Shrimp Fried Rice

From Art Museum Area   **Chinese**   *Serves 4*

Soy sauce, used extensively in Oriental cooking, is a liquid made from fermented soy beans, wheat and brine. It has a sweet yet salty flavor and comes in many varieties. This recipe calls for the light soy.

1 pound small shrimp, shelled
  and deveined

4 cups cooked rice

1/4 cup oil

2 eggs, lightly beaten

4 tablespoons soy sauce

Black pepper

3 scallions, finely chopped

1. In a wok or skillet, heat the oil and add the shrimp. Stir-fry for 1 minute. Add the scallions and cook for another 2-3 minutes.

2. To the shrimp, add the cooked rice, beaten eggs, soy sauce and pepper. Quickly stir-fry this mixture for about 3-4 minutes.

Vegetables

Cima di Rape
Broccoli Rape

From South Philadelphia   **Italian**   *Serves 4*

Broccoli rape is a member of the broccoli family. The stems are thin with small yellowish florets, and have a strong, slightly bitter flavor. Garlic and oil are traditionally used in this Italian dish.

1 pound broccoli rape, washed thoroughly, tips cut off stem (if stems are too thick, slice in half)

1/2 cup olive oil

2 large garlic cloves, minced

Salt and fresh ground pepper to taste

1. Blanch the broccoli and stems in boiling water for 1-2 minutes. Drain in colander.

2. Heat oil in skillet, add garlic and sauté gently for 1 minute. Add broccoli, cover and simmer gently for 8-10 minutes, or until the broccoli is tender. Serve at once with the oil and garlic used in the cooking process.

Serving suggestion: Italian broccoli goes especially well with roast chicken (page 107), lamb (page 122) or Chicken Wellington with Stilton (page 100).

Vegetarian Stir-Fry

From Kensington   *Serves 4-6*

This is a very unusual and tasty vegetable dish with a slightly nutty flavor and crunchy texture. Tempeh is an Indonesian soy food and is a good vegetarian substitute for meat. It is low in calories and has no cholesterol.

2 cups brown rice, cooked

1/2 package tempeh*

2 cups soy sauce

1 tablespoon vegetable oil

1 green pepper, diced

1 red pepper, diced

1 bunch broccoli, broken into florets

4 carrots, sliced

3 scallions, chopped

1 head cauliflower, broken into florets

1/4 cup toasted sesame oil

1. Cut the tempeh into small pieces and put into a saucepan. Add the soy sauce and simmer for about 35 minutes, stirring occasionally. The tempeh will absorb the soy sauce, becoming slightly sticky. Remove from heat. This mixture can be kept in the refrigerator for 2-3 days.

2. In a wok, heat the oil and stir-fry all the vegetables to desired doneness. Add the cooked tempeh and cooked rice. Mix well. Over high heat, quickly toss the vegetables and tempeh until heated, then sprinkle with sesame oil.

* Available at Oriental and health food stores.

Spanakopita
Spinach Pie

From the Northeast   **Greek**   *Serves 8-10*

Dill has a lovely mild flavor, and it complements the feta cheese in this wonderful do-ahead dish. Spanakopita may be frozen. To reheat simply defrost and place in a preheated 350° oven for 20-25 minutes, or until heated through. The phyllo dough may get soggy from refrigeration, but will crisp beautifully upon reheating.

3 10-ounce bags fresh spinach or 4 boxes frozen spinach

2 bunches scallions, cleaned, trimmed and chopped

1/3 cup olive oil

1/2 pound feta, crumbled

8 ounces cottage cheese

2 ounces cream cheese, cut into small pieces

2 tablespoons chopped fresh dill

1/4 cup pine nuts, lightly toasted (optional)

Salt and pepper to taste

3 eggs, lightly beaten

1/2 cup melted butter

15 sheets phyllo leaves

---

1. Wash spinach thoroughly and remove thick stems. Stew in as little water as possible, just until limp. Drain thoroughly, squeezing out any remaining water, and chop. *Note:* If frozen spinach is used, follow package directions for cooking. Drain thoroughly and squeeze out excess water.

2. Sauté scallions gently in olive oil until tender. Add to spinach.

3. Combine crumbled feta, cottage cheese, cream cheese, dill and pine nuts, if used, with the spinach mixture. Add salt and pepper to taste. Little if any salt may be needed, depending on the saltiness of the feta. Thoroughly mix in the beaten eggs.

4. Preheat oven to 350°.

5. Using a pastry brush, butter the bottom of a cookie sheet. Lay 8 sheets of phyllo in pan, one on top of another, buttering each sheet. Spread the spinach mixture evenly on phyllo. Cover with remaining 7 sheets, buttering each, including the top sheet. Place in the oven for approximately 45 minutes, or until the top is golden. Remove from oven, cool, and cut in squares according to the portions desired.

Stuffed Cabbage

From Manayunk   **Serves 4**

There are many different preparations for stuffed cabbage. This recipe calls for uncooked rice, but the long slow cooking ensures that it will be completely cooked through.

1 head of cabbage

1 pound ground beef

1 medium onion, finely chopped

1/4 cup uncooked rice

1/2 teaspoon salt

Freshly ground pepper to taste

2 tablespoons white vinegar

1 tablespoon sugar

1/2 cup tomato purée

1. With a sharp knife, remove the core of the cabbage.

2. Cook the cabbage in enough boiling water to cover for 20 minutes, or until soft. Remove cabbage to a colander to drain. Reserve cooking liquid. When cabbage is cool enough to handle, separate leaves gently and trim down thick stem on each leaf.

3. In a bowl, mix together the ground beef, onions, uncooked rice, salt and pepper.

4. Take 2-3 tablespoons of filling and place in center of cabbage leaf. Fold sides in and roll. Place seam side down in a deep casserole or Dutch oven. Continue until all of the filling and cabbage leaves are used. Make sure cabbage rolls are layered close together in the casserole.

5. Pour just enough of the reserved cabbage water over the rolls to cover the bottom layer, then add the vinegar. Mix the sugar in with the tomato purée and pour this over the rolls. Cover and cook on a low heat for at least 2 hours, or until leaf and filling are cooked through. Serve cabbage rolls with pan gravy.

Golabki
Polish Stuffed Cabbage

From Queen Village   **Polish**   *Serves 4*

Golabki are delicious and a meal in themselves.

1 medium head of cabbage

1 cup rice

2 1/2 cups water

1 large onion, minced

3 tablespoons butter or margarine

1 pound ground beef, or 1/2 pound ground beef and 1/2 pound ground veal or pork

1 egg

1 teaspoon salt

1/4 teaspoon pepper

1 garlic clove, finely chopped (optional)

1 15-ounce can tomato sauce

1. Remove core from cabbage. Place in a pot of boiling water to cover and cook for 10-15 minutes. Drain, cool and separate leaves. Trim down thick stem on each leaf.

2. Bring 1 1/2 cups of water to a boil and add rice. Over medium heat, cook rice for 5 minutes, or until it has absorbed all the water. Set aside.

3. Sauté minced onion in 3 tablespoons butter or margarine. Combine the meat, rice, onion, egg, salt, pepper and garlic (if desired). Mix thoroughly.

4. Preheat oven to 375°.

5. Place about 3 heaping tablespoons of meat and rice filling on each leaf. Roll the leaf, tucking sides either inside or under. Repeat with remaining leaves.

6. Place cabbage rolls close together in a baking dish or Dutch oven. Pour the tomato sauce, which has been mixed with 1 cup water, over the rolls. Cover and bake in the oven for 1 1/4 hours.

Variation: For cooking golabki on top of the stove, bring liquid to a boil, reduce heat and simmer for 1 1/4 hours or until tender. If desired, the cabbage rolls can also be dotted with 2-3 tablespoons of butter or margarine before cooking.

Kokt Rodkal
Red Cabbage

From the Swedish Museum,   **Swedish**   *Serves 4*
Packer Park

Molasses comes in light and dark forms and should be stored in a cool place. In this dish unsulphered molasses is used. The red cabbage in this recipe is moist and very flavorful and tastes even better heated through the next day.

1 large head of red cabbage, shredded

1 1/2 tablespoons butter

1 tablespoon molasses

1 apple, peeled and sliced

1 small onion, finely chopped

Juice of half a lemon

1/3 cup red wine vinegar

3 whole cloves

Salt and pepper to taste

1. In a large saucepan, melt the butter. Add the shredded cabbage and simmer, stirring occasionally for 5-8 minutes.

2. Add the molasses, apples, onions, lemon juice, vinegar, cloves, salt and pepper. Continue simmering for 1-1 1/2 hours, stirring occasionally, until the cabbage is soft and tender.

3. Before serving, remove the cloves and adjust seasoning.

Serving suggestion: Serve red cabbage with pork loin and prunes (page 111).

Lazanki
Cabbage-Noodle Casserole

From Port Richmond   **Polish**   *Serves 4*

Fat back is cured pork fat and needs to be fried until crisp to render away the fat. This gives a lovely flavor to this dish.

1 small head of cabbage, shredded
1/2 pound egg noodles

1/4 pound fat back, diced
Salt and pepper to taste

1. Cook the cabbage in water until soft, approximately 10 minutes. Drain well.

2. Cook the egg noodles according to package directions. Drain.

3. In a frying pan, sauté the fat back until well browned. Drain most of the fat away. Add the cooked cabbage and noodles to the sautéed fat back and toss together. Season with salt and pepper to taste. Heat through gently about 5 minutes and serve.

Serving suggestion: This would be good served with grilled kielbasa or any other spicy sausage.

Variation: For a slightly different flavor, add the same amount of pancetta* instead of fat back and brown as directed.

*Available at Italian specialty food shops.

Sauerkraut and Dumplings

From Queen Village   **German**   *Serves 4*

Sauerkraut is shredded cabbage preserved in a saltwater brine. Rinse the sauerkraut for a less salty flavor. Sauerkraut and dumplings are also good as a side course with sausages.

1 27-ounce can sauerkraut
1 country-style sparerib
1 large onion
Water

GERMAN DUMPLINGS
2 eggs
1 1/2 tablespoons vegetable oil
   or marrow from beef bone
1 teaspoon ice-cold water
1/2 cup flour
Salt and pepper to taste

---

1. To make dumplings, beat eggs well, add oil or marrow, water and flour, and mix until mixture resembles oatmeal.

2. In a large saucepan, place sauerkraut, sparerib and onion. Cover with water and simmer 1 1/2 hours. Remove sparerib and onion.

3. Add dumplings by 1/4 teaspoonsful and simmer another 45 minutes, or until dumplings are done.

Serving suggestion: Serve with roast loin of pork (page 108) or your favorite pork recipe.

Inlagda Rodbetor
Pickled Beets

From the Swedish Museum,   **Swedish**   *Serves 4-6*
Packer Park

It is easier to peel beets after boiling. They are a very colorful and versatile vegetable and in this recipe have a slightly piquant taste.

1-2 pounds small beets
1 quart water, or more to cover
2 teaspoons salt

DRESSING
1 cup white vinegar
4 tablespoons water
4 tablespoons sugar
2 cloves

1. Wash beets thoroughly and place whole in boiling water with salt. Cook until tender, about 30-40 minutes.

2. With a slotted spoon, remove beets from water. Cool slightly, peel and slice thinly. Place in a bowl.

3. Mix the vinegar, water, sugar and cloves together. Pour over the beets. Allow to marinate in the refrigerator for 1-3 hours or overnight.

Tzimmes
Honeyed Carrots and Sweet Potatoes

From the Northeast   **Jewish**   *Serves 4-6*

The Yiddish word Tzimmes *means a combination of meats or vegetables that are mixed together, as in this traditional Jewish dish. It is also very easy to prepare.*

1 pound carrots, scraped and
   thickly sliced

1 large sweet potato, peeled
   and thickly sliced

3/4 cup water

1/3 cup honey

1 teaspoon salt

1. Place the carrots and sweet potatoes in a saucepan and add water. Bring to a boil, cover with lid and let simmer for about 5 minutes.

2. Add the honey and salt. Simmer uncovered on low heat for about 30 minutes, or until the vegetables are tender. The water should evaporate slowly, leaving a nice glaze on the vegetables. The honey caramelizes so it does not seem overly sweet.

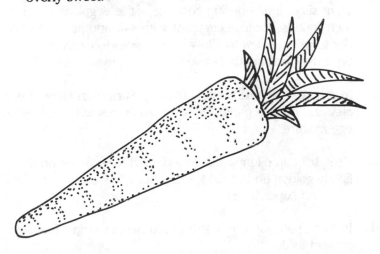

Melanzane e Ricotta
Eggplant with Ricotta

From South Philadelphia   **Italian**   *Serves 4*

Ricotta and mozzarella are two traditional Italian cheeses mostly used in cooking. In this recipe they are used with eggplant which turns this dish into an interesting variation of eggplant parmigiano.

2 large eggplants
Salt
4 eggs
1/2 cup Parmesan cheese
1/4 cup minced fresh parsley
2 large garlic cloves, minced
Flour
1/2 cup vegetable oil
1 green bell pepper, seeded and cut into strips

1 red bell pepper, seeded and cut into strips
2 cups crushed tomatoes
1 15-ounce container of ricotta
Freshly ground pepper
8 ounces whole-milk mozzarella, shredded

1. With a vegetable peeler, remove strips of eggplant skin at 1-inch intervals lengthwise. (This technique will hold eggplant slices intact during cooking.) Slice eggplant into 1/2-inch rounds. Sprinkle eggplant with salt and place in colander for 45 minutes to allow bitter juices to drain off. Squeeze slices gently between paper towels to dry.

2. In a bowl, combine 3 eggs, 1/4 cup Parmesan cheese, parsley and minced garlic. Dip eggplant slices in flour, then in egg mixture.

3. Heat 1/2 cup oil in skillet. Fry dipped slices in oil until lightly golden on both sides. Do not allow oil to burn. Drain slices on paper towels.

4. In same pan, sauté red and green pepper strips. Remove and set aside.

5. Pour crushed tomatoes into the same pan used for frying and simmer 10-15 minutes.

6. Combine ricotta, remaining 1/4 cup Parmesan and 1 egg.

7. Preheat oven to 350°.

8. Line a baking pan with half the eggplant rounds. Spread each round generously with ricotta mixture. Top with remaining rounds, forming eggplant/ricotta "sandwiches." Surround pan with red and green strips. Sprinkle mozzarella over eggplant and pour tomato sauce over mozzarella. Add several grindings of fresh pepper.

9. Place in the oven for approximately 15-20 minutes.

Polpettine di Melanzane con Salsa
Eggplant Balls in Tomato Sauce

From South Philadelphia   **Italian**   *Serves 4*

There are several varieties of eggplants including white and purple ones. Keep eggplants in refrigerator and use as quickly as possible. In this recipe use the larger purple eggplants. This is an interesting dish as the eggplant balls are very light and flavorful and a change from the traditional meatballs.

6 medium eggplants, peeled and shredded or finely diced

4 tablespoons grated macaroni cheese*

3 tablespoons shredded mozzarella

5 tablespoons fresh bread crumbs

2 garlic cloves, minced

1 tablespoon chopped parsley

Salt and pepper to taste

1-2 eggs

Flour

Oil

2 1/3 cups tomato sauce (page 220)

1. Preheat oven to 350°.

2. In a pan of water, boil the shredded eggplant for 2 minutes and drain. When cool enough to handle, squeeze as much water out as possible. Place in a bowl.

3. Add to the eggplant the cheeses, bread crumbs, garlic, parsley, salt and pepper. Mix carefully. Add 1 egg and mix again. If mixture feels too dry, add the other egg. The consistency of the eggplant mixture should be pliable enough to form balls easily.

4. Form eggplant balls about the size of walnuts, 1 inch in diameter. Flour the balls lightly before placing them on an oiled baking sheet. Bake in oven for 15 minutes, or until lightly browned. Transfer to an oven-proof baking dish and add tomato sauce. Bake 5-10 minutes.

*Macaroni cheese is a general name referring to Regianno Parmesan, Pecorino Romano or any Italian cheese used in cooking.

Calabacutas Rancheras
Zucchini with Chilies

From The Parkway   **Mexican**   *Serves 4*

Chilies come in several varieties. Some are very hot and should be used according to taste. Remember when handling chilies to wash hands well afterwards, or wear gloves.

1 pound zucchini, washed and
  sliced into rounds

Salt

1 tablespoon olive oil

2 green peppers

2 fresh green chili peppers or
  1 small can jalapeno chilies,
  seeded

1 onion, finely chopped

2 garlic cloves, minced

3/4 cup canned, frozen or
  fresh corn

1. Place the zucchini slices in a colander, sprinkle with salt and leave to drain for 20 minutes. Pat dry.

2. Heat oil in a skillet and fry the zucchini slices on both sides for 1-2 minutes, just until they are slightly browned.

3. Over a flame or in the broiler, cook the green peppers and fresh chilies until blistered and soft. Cool slightly and then peel, seed and cut into lengthwise strips.

4. Add a little more oil to the skillet and gently fry the onions and garlic until soft. Add the green pepper and chili strips together with the corn. Cover and simmer for 5 minutes. Uncover and simmer a further 5 minutes, then add the zucchini and salt to taste. Heat through quickly for 1-2 minutes more and serve. Do not overcook the vegetables. They should be slightly crunchy. For a hotter taste, add a few more chili peppers.

Serving suggestion: This dish goes especially well with pork.

Zucchini Parmigiano

From South Philadelphia   **Italian**   *Serves 4*

Italian parsley has a flat leaf and is more flavorful than the curly variety. It goes well in this interesting meatless alternative to the traditional parmigiano.

4 large zucchini, cut in half horizontally and sliced into 1/4-inch thick slices

Vegetable oil for frying zucchini and peppers

3 green peppers, seeded and sliced

2 eggs

2 tablespoons macaroni cheese

2 tablespoons fresh Italian parsley, chopped

1-2 garlic cloves, minced

Pepper to taste

SAUCE

2 tablespoons olive oil

1 large garlic clove, minced

1/4 cup fresh Italian parsley, chopped

1 fresh basil leaf (optional)

1 16-ounce can Italian plum tomatoes with juice, puréed in food processor or blender

---

1. In a large skillet, heat vegetable oil and fry peppers until crisp. Remove peppers and set aside. In the same skillet (adding more oil, if necessary), fry the zucchini slices. Remove and place on paper towels to remove excess oil.

2. Make a batter by combining eggs, macaroni cheese, parsley, garlic, and pepper. Dip the already fried zucchini in the batter and refry in hot oil until lightly browned. Put on paper towels to drain.

3. Make the sauce by heating olive oil in a saucepan. Add garlic and sauté 1 minute. Add parsley, basil and the puréed plum tomatoes. Cook approximately 20 minutes.

4. Preheat oven to 350°.

5. In a baking dish, place a layer of zucchini slices. Surround with the fried peppers. Pour some of the tomato sauce on top. Repeat layering using remaining zucchini. Top with tomato sauce and bake in the oven for 15-20 minutes, or until heated through.

Colcannon
Fried Potatoes and Cabbage

From Schuylkill   **Irish**   *Serves 4*

Traditionally eaten in Ireland at Halloween, colcannon is usually made with kale, but is sometimes made with cabbage. A plain gold ring or sixpence are often placed in the mixture. The ring means that the finder will be married within the year, and the sixpence predicts wealth.

1 medium head of cabbage or 1 pound of kale, shredded

4 potatoes, peeled and cooked

1 small onion or 6 scallions, finely chopped

1/4 cup milk

Salt and pepper

3 tablespoons butter

Fresh parsley, chopped (garnish)

1. In very little water, cook the cabbage or kale until tender. Drain and squeeze out as much water as possible.

2. Mash the cooked potatoes until very smooth. Mix in the cooked cabbage, onions, milk, salt and pepper.

3. Heat half the butter in a frying pan or skillet and add the potato mixture. Flatten slightly so it looks like a large pancake. Fry until the edges are crisp-looking. Dot the top with the remaining butter and run under the broiler for a few seconds until slightly browned. Sprinkle with parsley.

Serving suggestion: Colcannon goes well with grilled or poached sausages.

Latkes
Potato Pancakes

From Queen Village   **Polish**   *Serves 4*

Here is a classic potato pancake from Poland. Latkes are tasty and easy to make.

6 large potatoes, peeled and
  grated

1 large onion, grated

2 eggs

4 tablespoons flour

1 teaspoon salt

1/4 teaspoon pepper

Oil, enough to cover bottom of
  frying pan

---

1. Mix the potatoes and onions together. Drop in the eggs and mix well. Add the flour, salt and pepper. Mix thoroughly.

2. Heat the oil in a frying pan. With a tablespoon, scoop up some of the mixture and drop in the very hot oil, flattening the mixture slightly. Brown on both sides about 1-2 minutes.

Serving suggestion: Potato pancakes are very good served with sour cream or apple sauce, or with sugar sprinkled on top.

Papa Mahada
Mashed Potatoes

From Fairhill   **Puerto Rican**   *Serves 4*

This is a wonderful and versatile dish to use up any leftover potatoes, meat, or vegetables.

4-5 potatoes, peeled and
  cooked

5 tablespoons butter

1/4 cup milk, warmed

1 green pepper, chopped

1 whole chicken, cooked and
  shredded

Salt to taste

1. Place cooked potatoes in a large bowl and mash until very smooth. Add the milk and mix well. Then add the 4 tablespoons of butter and salt to taste. Mix thoroughly.

2. Fry the green peppers in the remaining butter and add to the mashed potatoes. Then gently mix in the shredded chicken.

Serving suggestion: Try this dish with mushroom gravy (page 217).

Tostones de Platano
Plantain Chips

From   **Puerto Rican**   *Makes about 15 chips*
Kensington

When plantains are ripe their skins should be quite black. This recipe calls for green ones, which are usually cooked and fried as in this recipe.

2 large green plantains, peeled   Vegetable oil for frying
    and cut into diagonal slices   Salt
Salted water

1. Soak the plantain slices for 30 minutes in cold salted water. Drain and pat dry on paper towels.

2. Heat 2-3 tablespoons oil in a skillet and sauté the plantain on low heat until tender, but not crispy. Drain on paper towels.

3. Lay a piece of wax paper over plantain slices and flatten slightly. Dip the slices into salted cold water. Pour into a sillet about 2-3 inches of oil and refry the plantain slices on both sides until crusty and golden in color. Dipping the slices into cold salted water, just before frying the second time, reduces the splatter of hot oil and crisps them nicely. Drain again on paper towels and serve.

Baked Beans

From Queen Village   *Serves 6-8*

This is a very tasty, straightforward no-fail baked bean recipe.

1 pound marrow or great northern beans

1/2 cup lemon juice

3 tablespoons molasses

Pinch of salt

1 tablespoon dry mustard

2 tablespoons Worcestershire sauce

1 tablespoon white vinegar

3-4 cups tomato sauce

1. Soak the beans overnight. Drain.

2. Preheat oven to 350°.

3. In an oven-proof dish, add the beans, lemon juice, molasses, salt, dry mustard, Worcestershire sauce, vinegar and tomato sauce.

4. Bake covered for 2 1/2 hours in the oven. If the liquid dries out too much, just add a little more tomato sauce.

Serving suggestion: A good accompaniment to sausages, frankfurters and baked ham.

Ful Medamis
Fava Beans

From Bella Vista   **Lebanese**   *Serves 4*

Generally legumes such as fava beans need to be picked through and cleaned of impurities. The packaged variety are fairly clean. They should be covered with a large quantity of water because they swell and absorb a great deal of it. Fava beans should be seasoned when they are tender or they become too soft.

2 cups dried fava beans, soaked overnight, or I can of fava beans

2 garlic cloves, crushed

Pinch of salt

1/2 cup lemon juice

1 small onion, finely chopped

1/4 cup olive oil

1/4 cup fresh mint, chopped

1/4 cup fresh parsley, chopped

1. Drain the dried beans. Place in a saucepan and cover with water. Cook until tender, about 1 hour. If using canned beans, pierce the top of the can, place in a pan of water and heat for 10 minutes.

2. In a large bowl, add the crushed garlic and salt together. Mix in the lemon juice, onions and beans with some of their liquid and the oil. Mix well.

3. Spread onto a large platter. Garnish with mint and parsley.

Serving suggestion: This dish should be served at room temperature with lots of pita bread wedges.

Arroz y Habichuelas
Kidney Beans and Rice

From Logan   **Cuban**   *Serves 4*

This popular Cuban dish includes sofrito—a mixture of chopped tomatoes, onions and garlic—and adobo, a spicy seasoning used in many Hispanic recipes.

1 cup white rice	1/2 pound smoked ham, diced
1 1/2 cups water	2 squash, diced
2 1/2 tablespoons vegetable oil	1 large potato, diced
1/2 chicken cube	1 teaspoon adobo seasoning*
Salt and pepper	1 tablespoon vinegar
1 19-ounce can red kidney beans	1/4 tablespoon tomato paste
1 teaspoon sofrito* (see page 221 for recipe)	

1. In a saucepan, add the rice, water, 1 1/2 tablespoons oil, half a chicken cube and a pinch of salt. Cover and simmer until rice is cooked, about 30 minutes.

2. In another saucepan, add the beans, sofrito, ham, all the vegetables, adobo, salt, pepper, remaining tablespoon of oil, vinegar and tomato paste. Fill half the empty bean can with water and pour into the saucepan. Stir to mix. Cook on medium heat for about 15-20 minutes, or until all the vegetables are cooked.

3. Serve over the cooked rice.

*Available at Hispanic food stores.

Navy Beans and Rice

From Fairhill   **Puerto Rican**   ***Serves 4***

This is a quick, easy and very tasty version of beans and rice.

1 pound dry navy beans,
  soaked overnight, or 1 large
  can of white beans

1 15-ounce can of tomato sauce

Salt and pepper

1 tablespoon oil

2 cups rice, cooked

1. In a saucepan, add the beans, tomato sauce, salt, pepper and oil. Bring to a boil, lower heat and simmer for about 1 hour, if using dry beans, or 15-20 minutes if using canned beans.

2. Season to taste with more salt and pepper. Serve over the cooked rice.

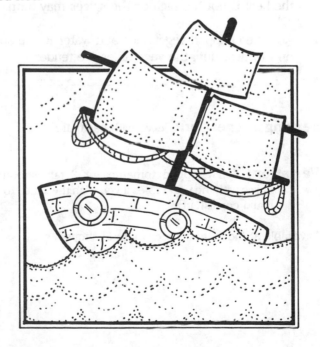

Sabzi Kari
Vegetables with Curry Sauce

From University City   **Indian**   *Serves 4*

Any seasonal vegetable may be used in this delicious dish.

4 tablespoons oil
1/2 teaspoon cumin seeds
1 onion, chopped
1-inch piece of ginger root
1 teaspoon coriander powder
1/2 teaspoon turmeric
1/2 teaspoon chili powder
Pinch of salt

1 cup coriander leaves (cilantro)
Variety of vegetables: broccoli,
  snowpeas, carrots, potatoes,
  (chopped)
1/4 cup water

1. Heat oil in a skillet and fry the cumin seeds for about 10-15 seconds, until they start popping. Add the onions, ginger, coriander powder, turmeric, chili powder and salt. Cook until the onions have wilted, stirring frequently. Make sure the heat is not too high or the spices may burn.

2. Add the chopped vegetables and water to the spices. Cook on low heat until the vegetables are tender.

Serving suggestion: Serve with basmati rice*

Variation: Add chopped tomatoes or 2 tablespoons of tomato purée with the vegetables if you wish the sauce to have a more liquid consistency.

*Available at Indian and specialty food shops.

Pasta, Noodles and Grains

Pasta Dough

From South Philadelphia

There is nothing more satisfying than making your own pasta dough, and it is not as difficult as you might imagine.

2 cups flour
2 eggs plus 1 egg yolk

1 teaspoon vegetable oil
Pinch of salt

1. On a clean, dry surface (preferably wooden), form a mound with the flour. Make a well in the center and put in the eggs, egg yolk, vegetable oil and salt.

2. Using a fork, gently scramble the egg mixture and very gradually incorporate the flour. Try to keep walls of flour in shape.

3. Proceed until almost all the flour is incorporated. When dough becomes thick, use your hands to blend in the remaining flour. (Toward the end of this procedure, scrap off any caked flour from work surface and hands.) Use fresh flour to dust on work surface. This will make a more tender pasta.

4. When dough is formed, knead 8-10 minutes until smooth and elastic. Cut dough into 6 pieces. (Dough not immediately being used should be covered to prevent drying.)

5. Feed dough 4-5 times through pasta machine set at widest opening. If dough becomes to sticky, flour lightly. Narrow the opening and pass dough through. Continue process, narrowing openings each time until dough is at desired thickness. Flour dough as necessary to prevent sticking and tearing. Cut to desired shape and allow to dry slightly before cooking.

Pasta Ambrosia

From Roxborough   *Serves 4-6*

This delicious pasta dish will bring applause. The combination of lobster, crab and shrimp gives it a delightful taste. If you omit the lobster meat, increase the amount of shrimp.

1/4 pound (1 stick) butter

2 tablespoons cold unsalted butter

1/2 cup chopped onions

1 green and red pepper, chopped

4 garlic cloves, minced

1/2 pound lobster meat, uncooked

1 pound shrimp, uncooked

1 cup fish stock

Salt and pepper

1 cup white wine

1 tablespoon cornstarch mixed with 2 tablespoons of water

1 pound pasta (see page 186 for homemade)

1/2 pound crab meat, picked through for shells

1. Heat a skillet until hot and add 1/4 pound butter. To this add the onions, red and green peppers and garlic and sauté until the onions are transparent. Add the lobster meat, shrimp and 1 cup of fish stock, and bring to a boil. Then add the salt, pepper and white wine.

2. Lower heat and cook for 5 minutes. To finish the sauce, add the cornstarch and water. Stir in thoroughly until thickened. Add the cold butter, one piece at a time. This will give the sauce a nice glossy look.

3. Cook pasta and drain.

4. Just before serving, fold the crab meat into the sauce and toss with the pasta.

Ziti con Melanzane e Zucchine
Eggplant and Zucchini with Ziti

From South Philadelphia   **Italian**   *Serves 6*

This is a lovely, hearty pasta dish. Fresh basil has a wonderful, pungent aroma and is particularly good in any tomato-based dish.

2 medium eggplants, sliced, salted and drained in a colander

1 cup bread crumbs

Oil for frying

1 large onion, chopped

2 garlic cloves

3 zucchini, sliced medium thick

1 15-ounce can of Italian plum tomatoes, drained

1 tablespoon fresh basil and parsley, chopped

Salt and pepper

1 pound ziti

1 4-ounce package of mozzarella, diced

1 cup Parmesan cheese

---

1. Squeeze excess moisture from the eggplant slices.

2. Place bread crumbs on a plate and bread the eggplants lightly. Add about 4 tablespoons of oil to a skillet and fry the slices on both sides until just browned. Remove and drain on a paper towel. When cool, cut into pieces.

3. Wipe out the skillet, add a little more oil and sauté the onions and garlic until slightly cooked. Add the zucchini and fry until lightly browned.

4. Add the can of Italian tomatoes, season with basil, parsley, salt and pepper. Simmer for about 15 minutes more.

5. Meanwhile, cook the pasta, drain and return to the cooking pot. To the pasta, add the eggplant pieces, zucchini mixture and mozzarella. Toss well.

6. Preheat oven to 350°. Pour the pasta into a baking dish, sprinkle with Parmesan cheese and bake for 20 minutes. Let rest for 2-3 minutes and serve.

Pasta con Spinaci e Ricotta
Pasta with Spinach and Ricotta

From South Philadelphia   **Italian**   *Serves 4*

This pasta dish is quick and easy to prepare, and the sauce has a tasty and creamy consistency.

1 cup cooked and chopped
   spinach, with excess water
   squeezed out

1 small onion, minced

2 tablespoons sweet butter

1 cup heavy cream

1 pound ricotta

1 pound pasta (shells, bows or
   your favorite shape), cooked
   according to package
   directions

1/2 cup freshly grated Parmesan,
   or to taste

1. In a saucepan, sauté the minced onion in butter.

2. Add the cooked spinach, heavy cream and ricotta. Stir and cook for about 3 minutes.

3. Combine cooked and drained pasta with spinach/cheese mixture and toss with Parmesan cheese. Serve.

Variation: Cook pasta. Mix together butter, ricotta and Parmesan cheese and toss into pasta. This is an adaptation of a Pasta Alfredo.

Seafood Pasta

From Spring Garden   *Serves 4*

*This is a delicious example of an Italian dish with French over-
tones. For a slightly different taste try using fresh sorrel, which is
sometimes called sour grass and adds a pungent flavor.*

3/4 pound large shrimp, peeled
  and deveined

3/4 pound bay scallops

7 tablespoons butter

3 tablespoons minced shallot

1 garlic clove, minced

2 tablespoons cognac

1 cup fish stock (page 39) or
  1/3 cup bottled clam juice

2 tablespoons tomato paste
  (optional)

1 cup heavy cream

3 tablespoons finely chopped
  parsley

2 tablespoons finely chopped
  fresh basil (other herbs can be
  used such as tarragon or
  coarsely chopped sorrel)

1/4 cup grated Parmesan
  cheese

2-3 fresh ripe tomatoes, peeled,
  seeded, squeezed of excess
  juice and chopped (optional)

1 pound fresh fettucini, cooked
  and drained (page 186 for
  homemade)

1. In a large skillet, melt 4 tablespoons of butter and quickly
sauté the shrimp and scallops until they begin to color,
about 3-4 minutes. Transfer to a bowl and reserve.

2. In the same skillet, add the shallots and garlic and cook
over medium heat for 2 minutes. Add the fish stock,
cognac, tomato paste, if desired, and the liquid from the reserved shrimp and scallops. Boil until reduced to about 1/4
cup. Add the heavy cream and gently boil until thickened,
about 5 minutes.

3. Add the parsley, herbs and cheese. Swirl in the remaining 3
tablespoons of butter. Add the reserved seafood and stir
just until heated through. Spoon over hot pasta. Garnish
with chopped tomatoes and additional cheese, if desired.

Spaghetti and Meat Sauce

From Mayfair   *Serves 4*

This is a tasty and easy way to make an old favorite.

2 tablespoons butter or
  margarine

1 onion, chopped

1 green pepper, chopped

1 pound ground beef

1 16-ounce can of Italian plum
  tomatoes

2 tablespoons tomato paste

1 garlic clove, crushed

1 teaspoon Italian seasoning

1 teaspoon oregano

1 pound pasta, cooked
  according to package
  directions

Parmesan cheese

1. In a skillet, melt the butter and sauté the onions and peppers until soft. Add the ground beef and brown.

2. Add the tomatoes and tomato paste with about 1/3 cup of water. Stir well. Mix in the rest of the ingredients and simmer for about 1 1/2 hours.

3. Serve the sauce over pasta and sprinkle with Parmesan cheese or put the cheese in a separate bowl for family or guests to help themselves.

Perciatelli with Genoese Onion Gravy

From South Philadelphia　　　**Italian**　　　*Serves 4*

In this unusual pasta gravy the flavor of the onions is subtle and sweet. Perciatelli, a thick, hollow spaghetti, has an excellent shape for this particular gravy. The gravy drains through the hollow and is absorbed by the pasta.

Vegetable oil

1/2 pound chuck or other stewing beef, left in one piece

3-4 pounds onions, peeled and quartered

1 stalk celery, scraped and cut into 1-inch pieces

1 cup water

Salt and pepper to taste

1 pound perciatelii

1/3 cup grated macaroni* cheese

---

1. In a Dutch oven or casserole, pour in enough oil to cover the bottom of the pan. Brown the beef on all sides. After the meat has browned nicely, add the onions, celery and water, and bring to a boil. Add a little salt and pepper to taste. Reduce heat to low, cover and simmer for approximately 3 hours. Remove meat from pan and reserve. Cool onion mixture.

2. Cook perciatelli according to package directions, drain.

3. Place the cooked onions in a food processor or blender and whiz 2-3 seconds. Return to pan and add cheese and heat, stirring occasionally for 1-2 minutes.

4. Place pasta on a large dish and cover with onion gravy. Sprinkle additional grated cheese, if desired. (The reserved meat can be cut into large pieces and served as the main course, or it can be shredded and served as a salad by adding 2 crushed garlic cloves, vinegar, salt and pepper to taste.)

*Macaroni cheese is a general name referring to Regianno Parmesan or Pecorino Romano cheese.

Lasagna

From Olney   **Puerto Rican**   *Serves 6*

This is a Puerto Rican version of lasagna. The sason and adobo seasonings in combination with the mozzarella and ricotta add zest to this traditional dish.

1 pound ground beef

1/2 cup dry red wine

1 teaspoon adobo* seasoning or 1 teaspoon of chili powder

1 garlic clove, minced

1 onion minced

1 envelope sason* seasoning or 1 teaspoon garlic powder and 1 teaspoon onion powder, mixed

1/4 pound mushrooms, sliced

1 teaspoon prepared mustard

1 15-ounce can tomato sauce

1 pound lasagna noodles

1 15-ounce container ricotta cheese

8 ounces mozzarella cheese, shredded

8 slices American cheese, Monterey Jack or Cheddar, cut into strips

1. In a bowl, add the ground meat, red wine, adobo, garlic, onion and sason seasoning. Marinate for several hours or overnight.

2. In a saucepan, place the marinated meat together with the marinade, mushrooms, mustard and tomato sauce and simmer for about 2 hours.

3. Cook lasagna noodles according to package directions and drain.

4. Preheat oven to 350°.

5. In a lasagna pan, pour about 1/2 cup of meat mixture in bottom and place one layer of lasagna noodles on top. Add another layer of meat mixture and then a layer of the three cheeses. Continue layering, ending with a layer of meat and cheese sprinkled on top.

6. Bake in oven for 30 minutes.

*Available at Hispanic food stores.

Baked Macaroni and Cheese

From Queen Village   *Serves 4*

Here is a deceptively easy macaroni and cheese. The use of cornstarch instead of a flour base makes this a lighter version than the more traditional recipe.

1 pound macaroni
1 1/2 cups milk
2 tablespoons butter

1 tablespoon cornstarch mixed with a little water to form a paste
3 cups New York aged Cheddar cheese, grated

1. Cook pasta according to package directions. Drain and leave in colander.

2. In the same pot the pasta was cooked in, heat the milk and butter. Stir in the cornstarch mixture and cook until slightly thickened. Add half the grated cheese and stir well. Then add the cooked macaroni to the cheese mixture.

3. Pour the macaroni/cheese mixture into a baking dish and sprinkle with the remaining cheese. Run under the broiler until cheese has melted.

Ziti con Polpettine
Beef and Veal Meatballs with Ziti

From Whitman | **Italian** | ***Serves 4***

Whenever you cook pasta add a drop of oil to the water; this will prevent pasta from sticking together. The combination of beef and veal makes a lighter meatball.

1/2 pound ground beef	1/4 cup finely chopped parsley
1/2 pound ground veal	1 tablespoon Romano cheese
4 slices white bread (crust removed), soaked in milk and squeezed dry	1/3 cup vegetable oil for frying meatballs
1 egg	1 recipe tomato sauce (page 220)
1/4 teaspoon garlic powder	1 pound ziti
1/2 teaspoon oregano	Additional freshly grated Romano cheese
2 tablespoons plain bread crumbs	
Salt and pepper to taste	

1. In a bowl, mix the meats, bread, egg, garlic powder, oregano, bread crumbs, salt and pepper, parsley and 1 tablespoon of Romano cheese. Mix well and form into balls about 1 1/2 inches in diameter.

2. Heat oil in a large skillet and fry the meatballs until browned all over. Remove and drain on paper towels.

3. Add the meatballs to the already simmering tomato sauce and continue cooking for about 1 more hour.

4. Cook the ziti, drain.

5. Serve the meatballs over the ziti with additional grated Romano cheese.

Variation: The meatballs can also be made with beef, veal or pork mixture, and would be great for sandwiches.

Meatless Baked Lasagna

From Whitman   *Serves 4-6*

This is a light lasagna with a delicate cheese flavor.

1 package of lasagna noodles, cooked al dente

1 15-ounce container ricotta

1 garlic clove, crushed

2 eggs

1 cup Parmesan cheese

8 ounces mozzarella cheese

Salt and pepper

Butter

1 recipe of tomato sauce (page 220)

1. Preheat oven to 350°.

2. In a bowl, mix the ricotta, garlic, eggs, Parmesan cheese, half the mozzarella and a pinch of salt and pepper.

3. Butter a lasagna pan and place one layer of noodles on the bottom. Spread a third of the cheese mixture on top and repeat layering 2-3 times, ending with a layer of cheese mixture.

4. Pour the tomato sauce over the top and sprinkle with the remaining mozzarella cheese. Bake in oven for 20 minutes. Let rest for about 5 minutes before serving.

Serving suggestion: Serve with a plain green salad and sliced radishes.

Egg Noodle and Spinach Casserole

From Frankford   **Ukrainian**   *Serves 6*

This is another simple dish that would go well as a side course with your favorite roast.

1 14-ounce package of egg noodles, cooked and drained

8 tablespoons (1 stick) butter

1 cup Swiss cheese, grated

1 teaspoon salt

1 cup finely chopped onions

3 pounds fresh spinach, washed and chopped

1/2 cup dry bread crumbs

4 hard-boiled eggs, quartered (garnish)

1. Preheat oven to 350°.

2. In a large bowl, toss the cooked noodles with 2 tablespoons butter, 6 tablespoons of cheese and salt to taste.

3. In a skillet, melt 3 tablespoons butter and sauté the onions until soft. Stir in the chopped spinach and cook uncovered for a few minutes.

4. Generously butter a lasagna dish. Place one-third of the noodles on the bottom and top with half the spinach. Repeat layering, ending with noodles on top.

5. Heat remaining butter in a small pan. Sprinkle the bread crumbs and remaining cheese over the noodles, then pour on the melted butter. Bake in the oven for 30 minutes or until the top is golden brown. Garnish with the hard-boiled eggs.

Cornmeal Bacon Dumplings

From Overbrook   **Soul Food**   *Serves 4-6*

Cornmeal was used by the Indians long before America was discovered. Cornmeal is made of ground corn kernels, and its texture can range from coarse to fine. In this dish the fine cornmeal gives the dumplings a softer texture.

1/2 cup flour
3/4 cup yellow cornmeal
1 1/2 teaspoons baking powder
Pinch of salt
1/2 pound bacon, diced and fried until crisp (drain, with fat reserved)

1/4 teaspoon Tabasco
1/4 cup chopped scallions
1 egg beaten
1/2 cup chicken stock

1. In a bowl, mix together the flour, cornmeal, baking powder, Tabasco and bacon bits.

2. In another bowl, combine the scallions, 1 tablespoon of reserved bacon fat, the egg and chicken stock. Add this to the dry ingredients and mix just enough to blend.

3. Bring a saucepan of water to a boil and drop tablespoons of mixture into the water. Cover and simmer gently for 10 minutes. Uncover and cook for a few more minutes, just enough to dry out slightly on top.

Serving suggestion: Serve with hog maws and chitterlings (page 118) or chicken and gravy (page 93).

Variation: Drop spoonfuls of the dumpling mixture directly into your favorite casserole.

Bulghur Pilaf

From Center City   **Armenian**   *Serves 4*

This unusual pilaf is very tasty. Bulghur is pre-cooked wheat kernels that have been dried and then ground into small pieces. Uncooked bulghur is best kept in a jar in the refrigerator for peak freshness.

4 tablespoons (1/2 stick) butter
1 cup fine noodles or vermicelli, broken into 1-inch pieces

1 cup bulghur wheat
2 cups hot beef broth

1. Melt the butter slowly in a heavy saucepan. Do not burn. Add noodles, and slowly, over low heat, brown them evenly, stirring gently. (Be very careful—the noodles tend to burn quickly if unattended.)

2. Add the bulghur and mix gently. Then add the hot boiling broth. Cover tightly and simmer until liquid has been absorbed, about 20 minutes.

3. Remove from heat and set aside, covered, for about 10 more minutes. Serve. (The pilaf can be put into a warm oven after it is cooked to keep it warm. It can stay that way until you are ready to serve.)

Serving suggestion: Bulghur pilaf goes well with meats and poultry, especially roast leg of lamb (page 122) and roast chicken (page 107).

Kasha and Bowties

From Bustleton   **Jewish**   *Serves 6*

This is a traditional grain dish. Kasha is roasted buckwheat kernels.

1 cup kasha, cooked according to package directions (Use the method utilizing chicken broth and egg in the cooking process.)

1/2 pound (8-ounce box) bowtie noodles

2 tablespoons vegetable oil

1 large onion, chopped

Salt and pepper to taste

1. Cook the bowtie noodles in boiling water for about 12 minutes, or until desired doneness. Drain in a colander.

2. In a skillet, add the oil and sauté the onion until lightly golden.

3. In a serving bowl, mix the cooked kasha with the bowties and add the cooked onion. Season with salt and pepper to taste. Toss lightly and serve.

Serving suggestion: Serve with roast chicken (page 107).

Hominy Grits

From Oak Lane   **Soul Food**   *Serves 4*

Hominy grits are made from hulled corn. They are white and about the size of toasted crumbs. When cooked, grits are fairly thick in texture and mild in taste. Try stirring in some Cheddar cheese to add a sharper flavor to this dish.

5 cups water

1 teaspoon salt

1 cup hominy grits

2 teaspoons sugar, or to taste

3-4 tablespoons butter

Freshly ground pepper to taste

1. Bring water to a boil and add salt.

2. Add grits, a 1/4 cup at a time, and stir constantly. When all the grits have been added, reduce heat and simmer covered for approximately 30-40 minutes, stirring grits occasionally to prevent sticking.

3. When all the water has been absorbed and the grits are done, add the sugar and butter and stir. Serve the grits in a bowl, adding freshly ground pepper to taste and additional salt and butter if desired.

Pizza, Quiches and Sandwiches

Pizza Dough

From Frankford   ***Makes 1 10-11 inch pizza***

This dough makes a crusty, chewy pizza. Yeast is a leavening agent that comes dry or in compressed cakes. Always make sure the water is lukewarm, not hot or cold, as this will kill the yeast. Also remember to check the expiration date on the package.

1 tablespoon yeast   Pinch of salt
1/2 cup lukewarm water   1 tablespoon oil
1 1/2 cups flour

1. In a small bowl, add the water and yeast and stir to mix. Cover with a cloth and let proof in a warm place for about 10 minutes or until foamy and bubbly.

2. Add the flour and salt to a larger bowl, mix in the oil and gradually pour in the yeast mixture. With your hands, knead the dough until it forms a ball and is of a fairly smooth consistency. Place in a greased bowl and cover with plastic wrap or towel. Let rise for about 1-1 1/2 hours, or until double in bulk.

3. Punch down and on a floured board, roll or pull into shape and place on a pizza pan or cookie sheet. Use your favorite topping or try "sici" pizza (page 206).

White Pizza

From South Philadelphia   **Italian**   *Serves 4*

*A few simple ingredients transform this into an unusual pizza.
You could serve this with your favorite soup or pasta recipe.*

1 baking sheet, 10x15 inches

Dough for 1 pizza (buy prepared dough or see page 204 for recipe)

2-3 tablespoons olive oil

Garlic powder to taste

Parmesan or Romano cheese to taste

Fresh ground white pepper to taste

1. Preheat oven to 375°.

2. Lightly oil baking sheet using a pastry brush.

3. Stretch dough to fit pan. Brush top of dough lightly with oil and season generously with garlic powder, cheese and ground pepper.

4. Bake in the oven for approximately 25 minutes, or until lightly golden. Serve at once.

Variation: To basic recipe, add chopped spinach, green and yellow peppers, tomatoes, sausage or pepperoni, or any other topping of your choice.

"Sici" Pizza

From South Philadelphia   **Italian**   *Serves 4*

This is a wonderful Southern Italian pizza. The combination of escarole, potatoes and Italian sausage makes this an outstanding dish.

1 baking sheet, 10 × 15 inches

Dough for 1 pizza (buy prepared dough or see page 204 for recipe)

2-3 tablespoons olive oil

1/2 cup tomato sauce

Freshly ground pepper to taste

1/4 pound escarole, washed, dried thoroughly, stems trimmed and chopped

1 medium potato, peeled, grated and patted dry

1/2 pound sweet Italian sausage, casing removed

8 ounces mozzarella, grated

---

1. Preheat oven to 375°.

2. Lightly oil baking sheet using a pastry brush.

3. Stretch dough to fit pan. Brush top of dough lightly with oil.

4. Spread tomato sauce evenly on dough and add several grindings of fresh pepper.

5. Layer pizza with escarole, potato, sweet sausage, and top with grated mozzarella.

6. Place in the oven for approximately 25 minutes, or until sausage is cooked through and pizza is lightly golden.

Lavosh Roll

From Center City　　　　　　　　　*Makes 8-10 slices*

Lavosh rolls are delicious and also make good hors d'oeuvres.
Lavosh crackers can also be served as is with cheeese.

1 large lavosh cracker

1 3 1/2-ounce package cream
　cheese, softened

3-4 tablespoons sour cream

Scallions, chopped

Tomatoes, thinly sliced

FILLINGS

Ham (cappacola, imported
　boiled, etc.), thinly sliced and
　chopped

Salami (Genoa, kosher, etc.),
　thinly sliced and chopped

Cheeses (provolone, Cheddar,
　Swiss, feta, etc.), shredded or
　crumbled

Olives, chopped

Pimentos, chopped

Roasted peppers, chopped

Green peppers, chopped

SEASONINGS

Oregano, basil, parsley, chervil,
　garlic powder, onion powder

Salt and pepper

---

1. Pass lavosh cracker under running cold water on each side
　　and place on towel. Cover with a second towel and allow
　　to soften, approximately 20 minutes. Cracker should be
　　flexible.

2. Carefully spread cracker with cream cheese/sour cream
　　mixture. Add your favorite combination of fillings.

3. Sprinkle with chopped scallions and layer with thinly sliced
　　tomatoes. Season to taste.

4. Roll lavosh carefully, jelly-roll fashion, and slice into rounds.

Chick-Pea Felafel in Pita
with Sour Cream/Tahini Sauce

From University City   ***Makes 8 pita sandwiches***

Tahini is an oily paste made from toasted sesame seeds. Blended with the other ingredients it gives this sandwich a Middle Eastern flair.

3/4 cup canned chick-peas, drained

1 green onion, cleaned, trimmed and finely chopped (include green part)

3 tablespoons tahini* (blend well before using)

1/2-3/4 cup finely grated carrots

1/2 teaspoon ground cumin

1/4 teaspoon cayenne pepper

Salt and pepper to taste

2 tablespoons vegetable oil

1 tablespoon sesame oil

4 pita breads, sliced in half, wrapped in aluminum foil and heated in a 350° oven for 10-15 minutes just before filling

Shredded lettuce

Chopped tomatoes

SOUR CREAM/TAHINI SAUCE

1 cup sour cream

2 green onions, cleaned, trimmed and chopped (include green part)

1 tablespoon tahini*

Dash or two of Tabasco

1. Prepare sour/cream tahini sauce. In a bowl, combine all ingredients and allow to stand for about 1 hour.

2. In a food processor or blender, purée the chick-peas coarsely. Put the purée into a bowl and add the carrots, green onions, tahini, cumin, cayenne, salt and pepper. Combine the mixture thoroughly and form into balls about 1 inch in diameter.

3. In a heavy skillet, heat the vegetable and sesame oil until hot, but not smoking. Add the chick-pea balls and fry, turning them very carefully, for 5 minutes or until brown.

4. Fill the heated pita breads with shredded lettuce and tomatoes. Add a couple of chick-pea balls and spoon about 2 tablespoons of sour cream/tahini sauce into each pocket. Serve.

*Available at Middle Eastern and specialty food shops.

Pepper and Egg Sandwich

From Pennsport   *Makes 2 sandwiches*

A classic sandwich, light and easy to make. The peppers add a splash of color to the eggs.

1 red and 1 green bell pepper,
  seeded and chopped

1 tablespoon vegetable oil

4 eggs, lightly beaten

Salt and pepper to taste

Hoagie rolls or whole wheat
  bread

1. In a skillet, heat the oil and gently fry the peppers until quite soft.

2. Add the eggs to the peppers and cook, mixing with the peppers, until scrambled. Add salt and pepper to taste.

3. Split a hoagie roll or use bread and fill with the eggs and peppers.

Variation: Add chopped onions to the peppers and fry together, or add grated provolone cheese to the egg mixture.

Zucchini Quiche

From Fairmount   **French**   ***Serves 4***

Here is a simple, tasty crustless quiche that is good for lunch or a light supper.

4 eggs beaten

1 medium onion, finely chopped

4 slices bacon or 1/4 pound ham, diced

2 zucchini, finely chopped

1 cup Cheddar cheese, grated

2 rounded tablespoons, self-rising flour.

1. Preheat oven to 375°.

2. In a bowl, combine all ingredients. The mixture will be fairly thick.

3. Grease a 9-inch quiche or pie dish.

4. Pour the mixture into the dish and smooth over.

5. Bake in oven for 30 minutes.

Serving suggestion: Serve with a green salad.

Sauces
and Stuffings

Homemade Mayonnaise

From Manayunk   ***Makes 1 cup***

Homemade mayonnaise is a must for certain recipes. The trick to making mayonnaise successfully is the addition of the oil in a slow, steady stream.

2 egg yolks

2 tablespoons lemon juice or white wine vinegar

1 teaspoon dry mustard or Dijon mustard

Pinch of salt and pepper

1 cup olive oil

1. In a food processor or blender, add the egg yolks, lemon juice, mustard, salt and pepper.

2. Process for 1 minute. Slowly add in the oil until the mayonnaise is thick and smooth. Keep covered in the refrigerator.

Serving suggestion: Use with old-fashioned potato salad (page 63).

Barbecue Sauce

From Fishtown   ***Makes 2 1/2-3 cups***

This will definitely become one of your favorite barbecue sauce recipes. You'll want to make it in large batches and freeze in individual portions to have on hand when needed.

1 15-ounce can of tomato sauce
    plus 3 tablespoons of water

3/4 cup brown sugar

1/2 cup red wine vinegar

1 garlic clove, finely chopped

1 onion, finely chopped

Salt

1. Pour all the ingredients into a large saucepan and simmer for 2 hours, stirring occasionally.

2. Cool, refrigerate and use as needed.

Serving suggestion: Place chicken pieces or spareribs in a baking pan, pour on sauce and bake at 350° until the meat is done.

Spicy Barbecue Sauce

From Port Richmond　　　　　　　　　*Makes 2-3 cups*

The pickle juice is the secret ingredient in this spicy barbecue sauce which will add a zesty touch to your favorite barbecue recipe.

2 cups finely diced onions
1/4 cup vegetable oil
4 garlic cloves, minced
1/3 cup molasses
1 15-ounce can tomato sauce
1/3 cup dill pickle juice

2 1/2 tablespoons Dijon mustard
1 cup cider vinegar
2 tablespoons Worcestershire
　sauce
1 teaspoon Tabasco

1. In a saucepan, heat the oil and sauté the onions until softened. Add the garlic and cook for about 2 minutes.

2. Add the molasses, tomato sauce, pickle juice, mustard, vinegar, Worcestershire sauce and Tabasco. Simmer for 30 minutes, stirring occasionally.

3. Cool the sauce and mix in a blender or food processor until smooth. For a slightly chunky consistency, reduce blending time.

Serving suggestion: Use as a sauce for chicken and spareribs.

Mushroom Gravy

From Tacony   ***Makes 1-1 1/2 cups***

This is a very versatile gravy. Use with your favorite beef, meat loaf or chicken recipe.

4 tablespoons butter

2 tablespoons flour

1 cup beef stock

1/2 pound mushrooms, cleaned and sliced

Dash Worcestershire sauce

Salt and pepper

1. Melt 2 tablespoons butter in a saucepan, add the flour and stir until well mixed. Pour in the beef stock slowly, stirring continuously until thickened.

2. In a skillet, melt the remaining butter and sauté the mushrooms until soft. Add the Worcestershire sauce, salt and pepper. Stir the mushrooms into the sauce and heat through.

Variation: Use chicken stock instead of the beef stock if you prefer.

Chili Sauce

From Fox Chase   *Serves 4*

A hearty chili that can be made as spicy or mild as you like by adjusting the Tabasco and chili powder.

1 pound ground beef
1 onion, chopped
2 8-ounce cans whole
   tomatoes, drained and
   squeezed

1 6-ounce can tomato paste
1/4 teaspoon oregano
1 bay leaf
Salt and pepper
1/4 teaspoon Tabasco
1 tablespoon chili powder

1. In an ungreased skillet, add the meat and onions, then fry until the meat has browned all over. Cover and cook until the liquid from the meat has evaporated, about 5-10 minutes.

2. Add the rest of the ingredients to the meat and simmer for about 1 hour.

Variation: Use as a sauce for pasta, chicken or hot dogs.

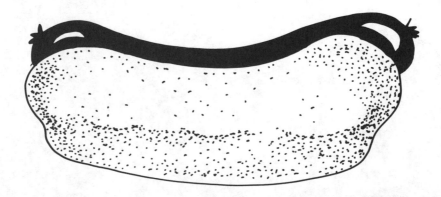

Horseradish/Sour Cream Sauce

From South Philadelphia   ***Makes 1-2 Cups***

This basic horseradish sauce can be used with a variety of foods, either meat or fish, and is excellent as a sandwich dressing.

1 1/2 cups sour cream
1 tablespoon Dijon mustard
1-2 tablespoons horseradish, or to
    taste

1. In a bowl, mix the ingredients together.

2. Refrigerate until chilled.

Serving suggestion: Serve with baccala fritters (page 10), or as a dip with raw vegetables.

Basic Tomato Sauce

From Fitler Square   ***Makes about 2 1/3 cups***

This recipe can be used whenever tomato sauce is called for in any of the dishes in this book.

3 tablespoons butter
2 garlic cloves, minced
1 15-ounce can tomato sauce

1 cup water
Salt and pepper to taste

1. In a saucepan, melt butter, add garlic and sauté 1 minute.

2. Add tomato sauce, water, salt and pepper. Bring to a boil, reduce heat and simmer 30-45 minutes, or to desired thickness.

Sofrito

From Fairhill   **Puerto Rican**   *Makes about 2 cups*

This is a quick and easy version of a highly versatile sauce that is used in many Hispanic recipes.

3 green peppers   2 garlic cloves
3 whole fresh tomatoes   1 tablespoon tomato paste
2 onions

1. In a food processor or by hand, chop the ingredients very finely. Do not reduce to a purée, as the vegetables should still be slightly chunky. Mix in tomato paste.

2. Place in a jar and refrigerate. Use whenever needed in any of the recipes in this book.

Gertrude's Oyster Stuffing

From Rittenhouse Square

Makes enough for a turkey of 10-15 pounds

This stuffing will become a family favorite at your table during the holiday season. Use your favorite combination of herbs. The rule of thumb is to use half as much of dried herbs as fresh.

4 tablespoons butter

1 large carrot, diced

2 medium onions, diced

2 celery stalks, diced

1 package unflavored toasted bread cubes

10-12 oysters

2 eggs

1 cup milk

Salt and pepper

1-2 tablespoons fresh herbs (rosemary, marjoram, sage, thyme, etc.) or 1 1/2-2 teaspoons of dried.

1. In a skillet, melt the butter and sauté the vegetables for 5 minutes. Add the bread cubes and oysters. Mix gently.

2. In a bowl, beat together the eggs and milk, then add the vegetables and oysters. Mix gently but thoroughly. Season with salt and pepper, then add the herbs.

Serving suggestion: Use as turkey stuffing or place in a covered baking dish, bake at 350° for 20 minutes and serve with roast pork.

Variation: To make a chestnut stuffing, use a 1-pound jar of whole chestnuts, chopped coarsely, instead of oysters.

Desserts

Hot Almond Soufflé

From Fairmount   *Serves 4*

The method of making an almond dough and using it to thicken the egg mixture is unusual, but you will find the soufflé very light and it won't fall quite so quickly.

3 tablespoons butter

3 tablespoons sugar

2 tablespoons flour

1 tablespoon ground almonds

1 1/4 cups milk

5 eggs separated

1/3 cup amaretto

Sugar for dusting soufflé dish

Confectioner's sugar for dusting
   finished soufflé

1. In a blender or food processor or by hand, knead the butter, sugar, flour and almonds together to form a dough.

2. Preheat oven to 350°.

3. Boil the milk, lower heat and add the soufflé dough in small pieces. Cook over medium heat for about 2-3 minutes. (This will thicken the mixture.) Turn off heat and let cool.

4. Add the egg yolks, one at a time, and then the amaretto.

5. Whisk the egg whites until light and foamy and gently fold into the soufflé mixture.

6. Butter a 1 1/4-quart soufflé dish and sprinkle with sugar. Pour mixture into dish and bake for about 20 minutes or until golden brown. Serve immediatley, lightly dusted with confectioner's sugar.

Gulab Jamun
Puffs in Syrup

From University City   **Indian**   *Serves 8-10*

This dessert is quite sweet, but light and delicious. Cardamom has a lovely, mellow, slightly lemony taste and is used quite frequently in Indian desserts. The pinch of saffron gives an interesting flavor and adds color to the syrup.

1 cup Bisquick

2 cups powdered milk

1/2 teaspoon cardamom powder

1 cup milk

1 cup vegetable shortening

SYRUP

2 cups sugar

3 cups water

Pinch of saffron

1. Prepare the syrup. In a saucepan, combine sugar and water. Bring to a boil and cook 2-3 minutes. Add a pinch of saffron and cook another 5 minutes.

2. To make the puffs, mix the Bisquick, powdered milk and cardamom in a large bowl. Gradually add milk to the dry mixture, a little at a time, to make a batter. Batter should not be too thick.

3. Heat the vegetable shortening and drop batter by teaspoons into the oil, a few at a time. Fry the puffs until lightly golden. Drain on paper towels and place in the syrup. (Puffs can be prepared ahead and refrigerated until needed.) Serve hot or cold.

Flan

From Logan   **Puerto Rican**   *Serves 8*

This short-cut version of the more traditional flan uses a few simple ingredients without sacrificing texture or taste.

2 large eggs, beaten   1 teaspoon vanilla
1 14-ounce can condensed milk   1 cup sugar for caramel
1 5-ounce can evaporated milk

1. Preheat oven to 350°.

2. Mix together the eggs, condensed and evaporated milk and vanilla. Set aside.

3. Make the caramel by placing the sugar in a saucepan and melting on medium heat, stirring occasionally. When sugar starts to form crystals, stir constantly until it redissolves to form a smooth caramel. It should be a medium-brown color. Do not cook to dark brown or caramel will be bitter.

4. In a 9-inch round cake pan, spread the caramel mixture evenly on the bottom by swirling the pan around. Work quickly as the caramel will harden. (When flan is cooking, caramel will melt.)

5. Pour the egg mixture on top of the caramel. Place the cake pan in a larger pan of hot water. Water should come 1/4-1/2 way up the cake pan. Bake for 40-45 minutes.

6. To unmold, go around the edges of the pie with a sharp knife and invert onto a serving platter. Chill several hours before serving.

Simple Rich Cholcolate Mousse

From Art Museum Area   ***Makes 4 3-ounce ramekins***

This is one of the easiest chocolate mousse recipes to prepare, and one of the most delicious.

5 ounces bittersweet chocolate

1 teaspoon instant coffee

1 egg, lightly beaten

Grated peel of 1 orange

1-2 tablespoons brandy, whiskey or Grand Marnier

Pinch of salt

3/4 cup scalded milk

1. In a food processor or blender, process chocolate until finely grated. Add the coffee, egg, grated orange peel, Grand Marnier (or liquor of your choice) and salt.

2. In a saucepan, heat the milk until scalded but not boiling.

3. Pour all at once into the grated chocolate mixture and process until smooth. (This is a quick and easy way of melting chocolate, as the hot milk melts the chocolate instantly.)

4. Pour into small ramekins or an attractive glass dish.

5. Refrigerate several hours to chill.

Irish Potatoes

From Schuylkill   ***Makes about 6 1/2 dozen***

Irish potatoes are traditionally made for St. Patrick's Day, but they can be enjoyed all year through.

8 ounces cream cheese, at
  room temperature

1/4 pound (1 stick) butter, at
  room temperature

1 teaspoon vanilla extract

1 14-ounce bag shredded
  coconut

2 pounds confectioner's sugar,
  or to taste

Ground cinnamon

1. Mix together the cream cheese and butter. Add the vanilla, coconut and sugar. With your hands, mix all ingredients thoroughly. Refrigerate for 1 hour.

2. Roll mixture into balls about 1 inch in diameter. Then roll the balls in ground cinnamon to coat all over. Refrigerate and bring to room temperature to serve.

Apple Crisp

From Art Museum Area   ***Serves 6***

A wonderful fall dessert made with good tart apples such as Winesap, Granny Smith or Rome.

8-10 large apples, peeled and
   thinly sliced
1 cup flour
1/2 cup sugar
1 teaspoon salt

1 teaspoon baking powder
1 egg
1/2 cup (1 stick) butter, melted
cinnamon

1. Preheat oven to 350°.

2. Place the apples in a 9-inch square baking dish.

3. In a large bowl, add the flour, sugar, salt and baking powder. Mix well. Add the egg and mix lightly with hands or a fork until crumbly.

4. Cover the apples with the crumb mixture. Pour the melted butter on top and sprinkle generously with cinnamon.

5. Bake for 30-40 minutes.

Serving suggestion: Serve warm or cold with vanilla ice cream.

Variation: Spread raspberries over the apples before topping with crumb mixture.

Chocolate Sour Cream Cake

From Fairmount   *Serves 10-12*

This is a moist and marvelous chocolate cake. Use a Dutch-process cocoa for an extra rich chocolate flavor.

3 layer-cake pans, 9 x 1 1/2 inches

3/4 cup cocoa

1 1/3 cups boiling water

1 cup (2 sticks) butter or margarine

3 cups packed light brown sugar

4 eggs

2 teaspoons vanilla

2 3/4 cups unsifted cake flour

3 teaspoons baking soda

1/2 teaspoon salt

1 1/3 cups sour cream

CHOCOLATE FROSTING

3/4 cup butter

3/4 cup cocoa

3 cups confectioner's sugar

6-7 tablespoons milk

2 teaspoons vanilla extract

---

1. Preheat oven to 350°.

2. In a small saucepan, add cocoa to boiling water and stir or whisk until smooth. Cool.

3. In a large mixing bowl, cream butter, sugar, eggs and vanilla at high speed until very light and fluffy, about 5 minutes.

4. Combine flour, baking soda and salt. Add to batter, alternating with cocoa mixture and sour cream, beginning and ending with flour mixture. Beat on low speed until batter is smooth. Pour into 3 well-greased and floured layer-cake pans. Bake for 35-40 minutes. Cool 10 minutes and remove from pans. Cool completely on wire racks.

5. Prepare chocolate frosting. In a small saucepan, melt butter over medium heat. Add cocoa and heat just until mixture boils, stirring constantly until smooth. Pour into a medium mixing bowl and cool completely. Add confectioner's sugar, alternating with milk, beating to a spreading consistency. Stir in vanilla.

6. To assemble, place one layer of cake, bottom side up, on plate and spread with frosting. Place another layer of cake on top of first layer, also bottom side up, and spread with frosting. Add third layer of cake, this time with bottom side down. Frost the top and sides of all three layers. Let sit for several hours before slicing.

Chocolate Ice-Box Cake Bunner

From Spring Garden

Serves 10-12

This makes a wonderful buffet dessert. Baking chocolate is available unsweetened, semi-sweet, bittersweet and sweet. To store chocolate, wrap well and keep in a cool place, not the refrigerator.

3 dozen small almond macaroons (preferably Italian macaroons), very finely crushed

2 squares (1-ounce each) of unsweetened chocolate, shaved

1/2 cup sugar

1/4 cup milk

5 egg yolks

5 egg whites

1 cup confectioner's sugar

1 cup butter

1 teaspoon vanilla

1. In the top of a double boiler, place the chocolate, sugar, milk and egg yolks. Cook stirring over boiling water until the mixture becomes smooth and thick. Remove from heat and cool.

2. Cream together the butter and confectioner's sugar and add to the chocolate mixture.

3. Beat egg whites until stiff. Fold into chocolate mixture together with the vanilla.

4. In a 10-inch spring-form pan, spread a layer of macaroon crumbs and cover with a layer of chocolate mixture. Keep layering, ending with macaroons on top. Refrigerate for at least 24 hours. (This cake should, if possible, be made 2-3 days ahead.) Serve with whipped cream if you dare!

Easy Chocolate Chip Cake

From Society Hill   ***Serves 6-8***

A simple cake with a brownie-like texture.

1 4-ounce package chocolate pudding

2 tablespoons milk

Butter

Flour

1 12-ounce package chocolate chips

1 package (2-3 ounces) chopped walnuts or pecans

1 box chocolate cake mix with pudding

1. Make the pudding mixture according to instructions on the package. Add the milk to the pudding mixture and stir thoroughly.

2. Preheat oven to 350°.

3. Butter and flour a 9-inch-square or round baking dish.

4. In a large bowl, pour in the chocolate cake mix. Add the prepared pudding mix and blend well.

5. Pour into the baking dish. Sprinkle chocolate chips and chopped nuts on top.

6. Bake for 30 minutes. Remove from oven and cool.

7. When cooled, cut into squares or wedges.

Pound Cake

From Fishtown   ***Serves 12 or more***

Vegetable shortening provides moisture and helps produce this incredibly delicious pound cake that is surprisingly easy to make.

3 cups sugar

3 cups flour

1/2 cup vegetable shortening

2 teaspoons vanilla or 1 teaspoon each vanilla and almond extracts

6 large eggs

1/2 pound (2 sticks) margarine

1 cup milk

3 teaspoons baking powder

1. Preheat oven to 350°.

2. In a large mixing bowl, combine all ingredients and beat at high speed for about 4 minutes.

3. Pour batter into a well-greased and floured 12-cup bundt or tube pan. Bake for about 1 hour and 10 minutes or until done. Top crust will be dark brown. Cool before removing from pan.

Variation: Add flavoring of your choice, such as orange or lemon extracts. For a slightly different taste, add 1/4 teaspoon mace.

Jimmie Cake

From Fishtown   *Serves 10-12*

Jimmie cake can be dusted with confectioner's sugar, iced with your favorite frosting or served plain.

1/2 pound (2 sticks) butter
2 3/4 cups sugar
6 eggs
1/2 cup sour cream
3 cups flour

1 teaspoon baking powder
2 teaspoons vanilla extract
Pinch of salt
1 package (3 1/2-4 ounces) jimmies

1. Preheat oven to 350°.

2. Cream butter and sugar together.

3. Add all the remaining ingredients (except jimmies) and beat well. Fold in the jimmies.

4. Pour batter into a well-greased and floured 12-cup bundt or tube pan. Bake for about 1 hour. (An inserted cake tester should come out dry.) Cool in pan for 10 minutes, then invert onto cake platter. Allow to cool completely.

Serving suggestion: Try a slice with a scoop of vanilla ice cream on top.

Cheesecake

From Rittenhouse Square

Serves 8-10

This rich cheesecake features an unusual cinnamon topping.

CRUST
2 1/2 cups graham cracker crumbs
1/2-3/4 cup butter, melted

FILLING
3 large eggs
2 egg yolks
1 1/2 pounds cream cheese, at room temperature

1 cup sugar
1 teaspoon vanilla extract
1/4 teaspoon salt
2 egg whites
Pinch of cream of tartar

TOPPING
Cinnamon
1 1/2 cups sour cream
2 tablespoons sugar
1/2 teaspoon vanilla extract

1. Make crust by blending crumbs with butter. Press into bottom and up sides of a 9-inch spring-form pan. Chill. (Begin with 1/2 cup butter: if crumbs do not hold together, add more butter.)

2. Preheat oven to 300°.

3. For the filling, beat the eggs and 2 yolks until thick. Add cream cheese, sugar, vanilla extract and salt. Beat until just smooth. In a separate bowl, whisk egg whites with a pinch of cream of tartar until stiff.

4. Fold 1/3 of beaten egg whites into batter (this will lighten batter), then fold in remaining egg whites. Pour into prepared spring-form pan and bake for 1 hour.

5. Remove cake from oven. Increase heat to 400°. Dust top of cake with cinnamon. Mix together sour cream, sugar and vanilla extract. Spread over top of cake. Return to oven for 5 minutes more. Cool on rack. Cover and refrigerate. Make at least 1 day (or, if possible, 2 days) ahead. Remove from spring-form and serve.

Individual Cheesecakes

From Manayunk   ***Serves 8***

These cheesecakes have a creamy soufflé-type consistency when eaten warm. Serving them individually on doily-lined plates creates an elegant presentation.

3 8-ounce packages cream cheese, at room temperature	1/4 teaspoon lemon juice
5 eggs	1 cup sour cream
1 1/4 cups sugar	1/2 teaspoon vanilla

1. Preheat oven to 300°.

2. Blend together the cream cheese, eggs, 1 cup of sugar and lemon juice until smooth.

3. Pour into foil-lined muffin cups or individual ramekin dishes. Bake for 40 minutes.

4. Meanwhile in a bowl, blend together the sour cream, remaining 1/4 cup of sugar and vanilla. Spread a little of this mixture on top of the cooked cheesecakes while still warm and bake for about 5 minutes more. Serve warm.

Chocolate Cheesecake

From Art Museum Area   *Serves 8-10*

The chocolate and coffee added to this dessert will please chocoholics and mocha fans alike.

CRUST
1 1/2 cups graham cracker or shortbread crumbs
4 tablespoons butter, melted
1 1/2 tablespoons sugar

FILLING
4 8-ounce packages cream cheese, at room temperature
1 1/2 cups sugar
3 large eggs, at room temperature

1 8-ounce package semi-sweet chocolate squares
2 tablespoons heavy cream
1 1/2-2 cups sour cream
1/2 cup double-strength cooled coffee
1 teaspoon vanilla

1. Make crust by blending crumbs with sugar and melted butter. Press firmly and smoothly into bottom of an ungreased 9-inch spring-form pan. (If crumbs will not hold together, add more melted butter.)

2. Preheat oven to 350°.

3. With a mixer, blend together the cream cheese, sugar and eggs. Beat on low speed just until smooth and blended. Do not overbeat mixture.

4. Melt chocolate over low heat with heavy cream. Add to cream cheese mixture together with sour cream. Pour in cooled coffee. Add vanilla and beat just until blended.

5. Pour and scrape batter into the prepared pan. Bake for 1 hour and 50 minutes. Center should remain somewhat soft, but will become firm on cooling. Let cake cool on rack for several hours. Refrigerate overnight, then remove sides of pan.

Ginger Cake

From Washington Square West　　　*Serves 8*

This is an unusually moist cake with very subtle hints of spices.

1/2 cup (1 stick) butter
1/2 cup sugar
1 egg
1 teaspoon cinnamon
1 teaspoon ground ginger
1/2 teaspoon ground cloves
1/4 teaspoon allspice
1/4 cup dark rum
1 cup hot water

1 cup molasses
2 1/2 cups flour
1 1/2 teaspoons baking soda
1/2 teaspoon salt

RUM SAUCE
1 cup (2 sticks) butter
2 cups sugar
1 cup heavy cream
1/4 cup dark rum

1. Preheat oven to 350°.

2. Cream together butter, sugar and egg until smooth and fluffy.

3. Add the cinnamon, ginger, cloves, allspice and rum. Beat until well mixed.

4. Add the hot water to the molasses.

5. Sift the flour, baking soda and salt into the butter mixture, alternating with the water/molasses mixture.

6. When well mixed, pour into a greased and floured 9-inch round cake pan. Bake for 50 minutes.

7. Prepare rum sauce. In a saucepan, add the butter, sugar, cream and rum. Cook until dissolved. Pour rum sauce over cake while still warm.

Oatmeal Cake

From Fairmount   *Serves 10-12*

Oatmeal gives this cake a pleasant chewy taste and texture.

1 cup oatmeal
1/4 pound (1 stick) butter
1 1/4 cups boiling water
1 cup sugar
1 cup brown sugar
2 eggs
1 1/3 cups flour
1/2 teaspoon salt
1 teaspoon baking soda
1/2 teaspoon nutmeg
1 teaspoon cinnamon

COCONUT PECAN ICING
6 tablespoons butter
1/4 cup condensed milk
1/2 cup brown sugar
1/2 teaspoon vanilla extract
1 cup shredded coconut
1/2 cup chopped pecans

1. Preheat oven to 350°.

2. In a bowl, soak the oatmeal with the butter and boiling water for 20 minutes.

3. Meanwhile, cream together the sugar, brown sugar and eggs.

4. Add the flour, salt, baking soda, nutmeg and cinnamon. Mix well. Combine with the oatmeal mixture and mix well again.

5. Pour batter into a buttered and sugared pan of 9 x 14 inches and bake for about 30 minutes. (Cake tester or toothpick should come out dry.)

6. To make icing, heat the butter, condensed milk and brown sugar in a saucepan until sugar dissolves. Remove from heat and add vanilla, coconut and pecans. Stir to mix.

7. Pour icing over cake while both are hot.

8. Place cake under broiler for 1-2 minutes, or until frosting is dark brown. Remove, cool and cut into squares.

Scottish Shortbread

From Center City   ***Makes 4 7-inch round cakes***

A very easy shortbread recipe that is traditionally made in Scotland around the holidays.

1/2 pound (2 sticks) salted butter
1/2 pound lard

1 cup plus 3 tablespoons dark brown sugar
5 cups flour

1. Preheat oven to 325°.

2. Using your hands, mix the butter and lard together thoroughly.

3. Gradually add the brown sugar and combine well.

4. Work in the flour slowly until dough is no longer sticky. (Dough should hold its shape and be soft.)

5. Divide dough evenly into 4 pieces. Using your hands, shape the dough into circles 7 inches in diameter and 1/2-inch thick and place in 4 7-inch pie pans. With a fork, prick the top of the shortbread cakes.

6. Bake for approximately 40 minutes or until golden brown.

Variation: If desired, shortbread can be made using all butter in the recipe and omitting the lard. Also, white sugar can be used, but the dark brown sugar gives it an especially good flavor.

Brownies

From Fairmount   *Makes approximately 8 squares*

Some brownies are like fudge, others are like cake. These are true brownies.

2 eggs
3/4 cup sugar
6 ounces semi-sweet chocolate
1/4 pound (1 stick) butter

1 tablespoon vanilla extract
1/2 cup flour
1 cup chopped pecans or
    walnuts

1. Preheat oven to 350°.

2. In a food processor or blender, cream together the eggs and sugar until light and fluffy.

3. In a saucepan, over low heat, melt the chocolate and butter together. Cool slightly, then add to the egg mixture and blend well.

4. Stir in the vanilla, flour and chopped nuts. Mix thoroughly.

5. Butter and sugar an 8-inch square pan. Pour in the brownie mixture and bake for about 30 minutes, or until a toothpick comes out clean.

Kruzdys
Love Knots

From Port Richmond **Lithuanian** ***Makes about 8 dozen***

These are quite similar to chrusciki and are sure to please.

12 egg yolks

1 egg white

2 tablespoons confectioner's sugar

2 tablespoons sugar

1/4 teaspoon salt

6 tablespoons sour cream and 6 tablespoons evaporated milk (or 9 tablespoons sour cream and 3 tablespoons regular milk)

1/2 teaspoon vanilla extract, whiskey or brandy

6 cups flour

Oil for frying

Additional confectioner's sugar for dusting

1. Beat egg yolks until light and frothy. Add egg white and beat until mixed.

2. Add the remaining ingredients with a little of the flour. Mix and gradually add about 2 more cups of flour. The dough will be a little sticky at this point.

3. Sprinkle a little more of the flour on the table and place the batter mixture on top. Gradually mix in the other 3 1/2-4 cups of flour, kneading for about 5-8 minutes. Let the dough rest for 10 minutes.

4. On a floured board, roll out the dough to about 1/8-inch thickness, dusting the board frequently to prevent sticking. Roll the dough into a rectangular shape. Cut the rectangle into long strips about 2 inches wide. About every 2 inches, cut the strips diagonally to form rows of diamond shapes. Make a 1-inch slit lengthwise in the center of each diamond. Then push one end of the diamond through the slit to make a knot.

5. In a heavy skillet, heat oil (about 2 inches deep) and fry the knots until lightly browned on one side. Then turn and fry the other side. Drain on paper towels. Cool and dust with confectioner's sugar.

Chrusciki
Fried Bowties with Powdered Sugar

From Queen Village   **Polish**   ***Makes about 5 dozen***

These are well worth the effort to make and will melt in your mouth.

1 1/4 cups flour

2 tablespoons confectioner's sugar

6 egg yolks

1 tablespoon rum or brandy

1-2 tablespoons sour cream

1 teaspoon vanilla extract

1/4 teaspoon salt

1 1/2 pounds vegetable shortening for frying

Additional confectioner's sugar for dusting

1. On a table or other flat surface, combine flour and confectioner's sugar. Make a well in the center and add remaining ingredients. Using a fork, gradually work the flour into the ingredients. When a dough is formed, knead with your hands for about 8 minutes until dough is smooth. Cut dough in half, cover and set half aside to prevent drying.

2. Using a rolling pin, roll out dough to about 1/8-inch thickness, dusting surface with flour occasionally as you roll to prevent sticking. Roll dough into a roughly rectangular shape. Slice the rectangle into long strips about 2 inches wide. About every 2 inches, cut the strips diagonally to create a series of diamond shapes. Make a 1-inch slit lengthwise in the center of each diamond. Then push one end of the diamond through the slit to make a bowtie.

3. In a heavy skillet, melt the shortening and fry the bowties until golden yellow on one side. Then turn and fry the other side. Be careful not to brown or cook too quickly. Remove and drain on paper towels. Cool and dust with confectioner's sugar.

Schnecken

From Art Museum Area   **Jewish**   ***Makes about 60***

These delectable little pastries are delicious served with coffee or afternoon tea.

1/2 pound (2 sticks) butter, softened

1/2 cup sour cream

1 egg yolk

2 cups flour

1 cup sugar mixed with 2 teaspoons ground cinnamon

ORANGE MARMALADE FILLING

1 cup orange marmalade

1 cup raisins

1 cup walnuts, finely chopped

1. Combine butter, sour cream and egg yolk. Add flour to form dough. Divide dough into four balls and refrigerate overnight.

2. Allow refrigerated dough to soften slightly at room temperature before rolling.

3. To make filling: Combine marmalade, raisins and walnuts in a bowl. Set aside.

4. Sprinkle a fourth of the cinnamon/sugar mixture on a pastry board or flat surface. Roll out first ball of dough on top of mixture. With a sharp knife, cut the dough into small pie-shaped wedges (about 15 wedges per ball).

5. Preheat oven to 350°.

6. Place 1/2 teaspoon of filling on each wedge and roll into small crescent shapes. Repeat with remaining balls. (When rolling into crescents, some of the filling will escape and coat the outer surface of the crescent. Do not wipe away, just place them on cookie sheet as is.)

7. Bake on an ungreased cookie sheet for 30 minutes. (Two cookie sheets can be used to bake schnecken all at once; but watch carefully—they burn easily.)

Hamentashen

From the Northeast   **Jewish**   *Makes about 50*

The three points of these triangular cookies represent the patriarchs of Judaism—Abraham, Isaac and Jacob.

1 cup sugar

1 cup vegetable oil

4 eggs

1/4 teaspoon salt

2 1/2 teaspoons baking powder

2 teaspoons vanilla extract

3 cups flour

Beaten egg for egg wash

FILLINGS
Chopped prunes or apricots

Preserves or pie filling

Poppy seed

1. Preheat oven to 375°.

2. Mix together the sugar, oil, eggs, salt, baking powder and vanilla extract.

3. Add enough flour to form a soft dough that does not stick to hands.

4. Roll out dough, but not too thinly. Using a glass with a lightly floured rim, cut out circles about 3 inches across. Place a teaspoon of filling in the center of each. (For poppy seed filling, mix together 1/2 cup poppy seeds, 1 cup finely chopped walnuts and 3/4 cup raisins [optional]. Add enough honey to hold filling together.) Bring up the sides of each circle to form a triangle with the filling showing in the center. Crimp edges closed by pinching.

5. Place on an ungreased cookie sheet. Brush top and sides with beaten egg wash. Bake for approximately 15-20 minutes or until golden brown. Leftover dough scraps can be pressed together and rerolled.

Variation: For cookies, roll out dough and use cookie cutters. Sprinkle with cinnamon and sugar and bake until golden brown.

Biscotti

From South Philadelphia   **Italian**   ***Makes about 50 cookies***

These traditional Italian cookies are easy to make and truly delicious. The anise gives them a pleasant licorice flavor.

5 cups flour

1 cup sugar

5 teaspoons baking powder

5 eggs

1/2 pound margarine, melted

1 teaspoon vanilla extract

1 drop anise oil, 1 teaspoon anisette or 1 teaspoon crushed aniseed

1. Preheat oven to 350°.

2. Put flour, sugar and baking powder in a large bowl and mix together.

3. Make a well in the center of the dry mixture and add in the eggs, margarine, vanilla extract and anise flavoring. With a fork, beat the liquid ingredients first. Then gradually blend together with the dry ingredients to form a dough. Knead lightly.

4. Cut dough into 4 parts and shape each into a loaf. Place on an ungreased cookie sheet, leaving room between loaves to expand. Bake for about 25 minutes or until lightly browned. Remove and cool for 5-10 minutes.

5. Using a sharp knife, carefully cut each loaf into 1/2-inch slices. Place slices back on cookie sheet, standing up about 1 inch apart. Bake 10-15 minutes longer to lightly toast. Remove and allow to cool. Store in a tightly covered container.

Serving suggestion: These cookies are very nice with morning coffee or tea and are especially good to have on hand for guests.

Brown-Edge Wafers

From Art Museum Area   *Makes about 54 wafers*

These wafers are thin, crisp and so very simple to make. You'll never have enough on hand.

3/4 cup butter or margarine, softened

1 cup sugar

1 egg

1 1/2 cups unsifted all-purpose flour

4 ounces slivered almonds, finely chopped

Grated rind of 2 lemons

---

1. Preheat oven to 350°.

2. In a bowl, mix together the butter, sugar and egg.

3. Stir in the flour, almonds and grated lemon rind.

4. Shape into about 54 balls. Place on greased cookie sheets. With floured fingers, press each into thin 3-inch rounds.

5. Bake for about 10-12 minutes or until edges are brown. Cool for 30 seconds on cookie sheets, then cool on racks. Cookies should be stored in an airtight container in a cool, dry place.

Serving suggestion: These wafers are a wonderful addition to afternoon tea or as a special garnish with your favorite ice cream.

Rick's Lemon Bars

From Fairmount   ***Makes about 20 squares***

Good and crunchy with a lovely lemon flavor.

1/2 cup (1 stick) butter

1 cup flour plus 2 tablespoons
 flour for lemon filling

1/4 cup confectioner's sugar

2 large eggs

3/4 cup sugar

1/4 teaspoon salt

1/2 teaspoon baking powder

2-4 tablespoons fresh lemon juice

Additional confectioner's sugar
 for dusting

1. Preheat oven to 350°.

2. Cream the butter. Add 1 cup of flour and 1/4 cup confectioner's sugar and blend until mixture resembles coarse
   crumbs. Press mixture into the bottom of an 8-inch square
   pan. Bake for 20 minutes until lightly golden.

3. Beat the eggs in a bowl. Add the sugar, salt, baking powder,
   lemon juice and remaining 2 tablespoons flour and mix
   thoroughly. Pour this mixture over the hot dough and bake
   another 25 minutes or until golden.

4. Sprinkle with confectioner's sugar and cut into 2-inch
   squares before totally cool.

Mexican Wedding Cakes

From Fishtown   *Makes about 48 cookies*

These are "melt-in-your-mouth" cookies.

1 cup butter, at room
　temperature
1/2 cup confectioner's sugar
1 teaspoon vanilla

2 cups flour
1/4 cup walnuts, finely chopped
3/4 cup confectioner's sugar for
　dusting

1. Preheat oven to 400°.

2. In a large bowl, food processor or blender, beat the butter, sugar and vanilla together.

3. Work enough of the flour into the mixture so that it holds together. Stir in the nuts.

4. Divide the mixture into 4 equal parts, then divide each part into 12 pieces. Roll each piece into a small ball.

5. Place on an ungreased cookie sheet and bake for 10 minutes. Do not allow cookies to brown.

6. While still hot, toss one at a time in the confectioner's sugar. The sugar melts to form a slight glaze.

7. Set cookies to cool on a platter. When cool, roll cookies in additional confectioner's sugar.

Poached Pears with Caramel Sauce

From Fairmount   ***Serves 8***

This is an irresistible dessert and a wonderful ending to a dinner party. Firm bosc pears work best in this recipe.

8 firm pears, peeled and cored
    from the bottom, retaining
    stem

4 cups water

3 cups sugar

Juice of half a lemon

CARAMEL SAUCE
3/4 cup sugar

1 cup heavy cream

GARNISH
Grated zest of 1 lemon

---

1. In a saucepan large enough to hold the 8 pears comfortably, bring to a boil the water, sugar and lemon juice. Reduce heat and simmer for 15-20 minutes.

2. Add the pears to the syrup, cover and poach gently for 20-30 minutes, depending on ripeness. Remove saucepan from heat and keep pears in the syrup until ready to serve.

3. To make caramel sauce, place the sugar in a heavy saucepan and cook over medium heat until the sugar dissolves and caramelizes to a brown color. Very carefully and gently, pour the heavy cream into the pan and reboil until sauce is smooth and slightly thickened.

4. To serve, drain the pears, place on serving plates and pour on some of the caramel sauce. Garnish with lemon zest. (To make pears stand upright, simply slice a thin layer off the bottom of each pear to make a flat surface.)

Serving suggestion: For a special touch and a splash of color, add a few fresh raspberries for garnish.

Variation: To make a chocolate sauce for pears, combine 8 ounces bittersweet chocolate (chopped), 5 tablespoons butter, 1/2 cup heavy cream and 2 tablespoons water in a heavy saucepan. Simmer until sauce is thick and smooth. Remove from heat and stir in 2 teaspoons vanilla extract.

Butter Cookies

From Fishtown   *Makes about 2 1/2-3 dozen cookies*

An excellent recipe. These are butter cookies to be proud of.

1 pound butter, at room
  temperature
1 1/3 cups sugar
1/2 teaspoon vanilla extract

1 teaspoon lemon juice
Pinch of salt
2 eggs
4 1/2 cups flour

1. Preheat oven to 350°.

2. Cream butter and add sugar a little at a time. Mix well.

3. Add vanilla, lemon juice and salt and continue beating.

4. Add eggs, one at a time, beating well after each addition.

5. Mix in flour. Put cookie batter in a cookie press and press out onto an ungreased cookie sheet. (To make by hand, simply pinch off a small piece of dough, roll to form a ball and flatten slightly. Place on an ungreased cookie sheet.)

6. Bake cookies for 15-20 minutes, or until edges brown lightly. Do not allow cookies to get too brown.

Variation: For an interesting twist, place a pecan half in the center of each cookie before baking.

Easter Cookies

From South   **Italian**   ***Makes about 4 dozen slices***
Philadelphia

These traditional cookies are enjoyed by family and friends during the Easter holiday season.

6 eggs

6 teaspoons baking powder

1/4 cup vegetable oil

1 5-ounce can evaporated milk

2 cups sugar

2 teaspoons vanilla extract

4 tablespoons butter, softened

7-8 cups flour

2 13-ounce jars jelly or preserves
(strawberry, cherry, black
currant, etc.)

1. Preheat oven to 350°.

2. In a bowl, add the eggs, baking powder, oil, evaporated milk, sugar, vanilla and butter. Mix well. Add the flour, a little at a time, until a soft dough forms. (Dough should no longer stick to hands.) Cut dough into 4 pieces. Work with one piece at a time, keeping remaining dough covered to prevent drying.

3. On a well-floured surface, pat one piece of dough to form a rectangular shape (9x12 inches and 1/4-inch thick). Spread a layer of jelly over half the dough and fold the other half over the jelly. Seal ends by pressing dough together with fingers.

4. Bake on a cookie sheet for approximately 15-20 minutes or until lightly browned. Cool and cut into slices about 1/2-inch wide.

Kourkoubini
Walnut Cookies in Syrup

From the Northeast   **Greek**   ***Makes about 40 cookies***

Farina (also called semolina) is used in many popular Greek desserts. It imparts a slightly nut-like texture in these syrup-soaked cookies.

1 1/2 cups vegetable oil

1/4 pound (1 stick) butter

1/3 cup uncooked farina

1/3 cup freshly squeezed orange juice

1 tablespoon baking powder

1/2 teaspoon baking soda

1/3 cup granulated sugar

3 tablespoons whiskey

5-6 cups flour

1 cup ground walnuts

SYRUP

3 cups sugar

3 cups water

14 whole cloves

1 cinnamon stick

1 slice lemon

1 tablespoon honey

1. Prepare syrup. In a medium-size saucepan, combine all ingredients except honey. Bring to a boil, reduce heat and simmer for 20-25 minutes, or until reduced to about 2 2/3 cups. Add the honey and simmer another 5-10 minutes. Reserve. Before using, remove lemon slices, cloves and cinnamon stick.

2. To make the cookies, begin by heating the oil in a medium-size saucepan for 5 minutes over moderate heat. Reduce heat to low, add butter and cook until melted. Remove from heat and stir in farina. Allow to stand 1 hour.

3. In a large bowl, mix together orange juice, baking powder and baking soda. (Mixture will start to foam.) Stir in farina mixture, sugar and whiskey.

4. Add the flour, one cup at a time, mixing well after each addition until a firm, smooth dough is formed (add more flour, if necessary).

5. Preheat oven to 350°.

6. Using about 2 full tablespoons, form dough into egg shapes. Place about 2 inches apart on an ungreased cookie sheet and flatten very slightly. Bake for 20-25 minutes or until lightly browned. Remove from oven and cool for at least 1 hour.

7. Heat syrup and dip cookies in syrup. Drain and sprinkle with ground walnuts. Cool cookies several hours before serving. This allows them to absorb the syrup.

Cream Cheese Pastry Crust

From Strawberry Mansion   ***Makes 1 8-inch pie crust***

This is a fool-proof pastry crust and can be used with any of your favorite pie recipes.

1 stick butter
1 4-ounce package cream
  cheese

1/2 cup flour
Pinch of salt

1. In a food processor or blender, cream together the butter and cream cheese until well combined.

2. Gradually add the flour and salt. Mix until a soft dough forms.

3. Roll out dough on a floured board.

Basic Pie Crust

From Queen Village   *Makes 1 10-inch crust*

For a light flaky crust, do not handle the dough more than is necessary. When blending flour and shortening, be sure there are bits of shortening left in the dough resembling coarse crumbs.

1 1/2 cups flour

Pinch of salt

Pinch of sugar (optional)

5 1/2 tablespoons butter, chilled
  and cut into pieces

3 tablespoons vegetable
  shortening, chilled

Cold water (3-4 tablespoons)

With food processor:

1. Place flour, salt, sugar (if used), butter and shortening in processor bowl fitted with a steel blade. Whiz 6-7 times, or until coarse crumbs form.

2. Dribble in cold water and process just until a ball forms. (Dough will pull away from sides and come toward blade.) Remove and allow to rest 10-15 minutes, then roll out on a floured surface.

By hand:

1. In a bowl, toss together the flour, salt and sugar (if used). With a pastry blender or by hand, cut in butter and shortening until coarse crumbs form.

2. Dribble in water and blend with a fork until clumps of dough start to hold together. Using your hands, gather dough and form into a ball. Allow to rest 10-15 minutes, then roll out on a floured surface.

Pecan Pie

From Queen Village   ***Serves 8***

There are many versions of pecan pie, but this is one of Philadelphia's best.

1 10-inch pie crust (page 260)

FILLING
1 cup dark brown sugar
1/3 teaspoon salt
4 eggs
1 1/2 cups dark corn syrup

1/2 teaspoon vanilla extract
1 tablespoon dark rum
1/4 cup molasses
1 1/2 cups pecan halves

1. Preheat oven to 350°.

2. In a bowl, mix together the brown sugar and salt.

3. In a separate bowl, mix eggs, corn syrup, vanilla, rum and molasses.

4. Mix the dry ingredients with the wet mixture.

5. Place pecans into the pie crust, then pour the filling over the pecans. Bake for 45-50 minutes. When pie is cooked, it should be slightly runny and may have little cracks in it. It will harden and even out when cooled.

Fudge Pie

From Chestnut Hill   *Serves 6*

An irresistible chocolate dessert that is really quite simple to make.

2 ounces unsweetened
   chocolate
1/4 pound (1 stick butter) butter
1 cup sugar
2 eggs, separated

1/3 cup flour
1 teaspoon vanilla extract
Pinch of salt

1. Preheat oven to 325°.

2. In a saucepan, over low heat, gently melt the chocolate and butter. Remove from heat and cool slightly.

3. Stir in the sugar, egg yolks, flour and vanilla.

4. Beat egg whites until stiff peaks form, add a pinch of salt and beat again briefly. Fold into the chocolate mixture.

5. Pour into a 9-inch pie dish and bake for 30 minutes. Serve warm or cold.

Serving suggestion: This pie is especially good served warm with vanilla ice cream.

Variation: Pour chocolate mixture into a graham cracker crust and bake as instructed above.

Mazarintarta
Marzipan Tarts

From the Swedish Museum,   **Swedish**   *Makes 4 tarts*
Packer Park

These tarts are delicate and delicious. Use the easy almond filling in any recipe that calls for marzipan.

CRUST
1/2 cup (1 stick) unsalted butter
1/4 cup confectioner's sugar
1 egg yolk
1 cup flour

ALMOND FILLING
1/2 cup sugar
1/3 cup butter
2/3 cup blanched almonds,
     finely ground
2 eggs
Confectioner's sugar for sprinkling

1. Prepare almond filling. In the bowl of a food processor, beat the sugar and butter until smooth, then add the ground almonds and eggs. Mix until well blended.

2. Preheat oven to 250°.

3. In a bowl, beat together the butter and sugar until light and fluffy. Add the egg yolk and flour. Mix until a soft dough is formed.

4. Butter tart molds. Roll out the dough and line molds with the pastry.

5. Pour in the filling and spread evenly into the shells. Bake for 30 minutes. The tarts should be light golden in color.

6. Cool the tarts and remove very carefully (the pastry is very fragile). Sprinkle top with confectioner's sugar and serve warm or at room temperature.

Variation: The filling can be put into an 8-inch pie dish, baked and cut into wedges.

Lemon and Strawberry Meringue Tart

From Society Hill   *Serves 8-12*

*This spectacular dessert is lovely to look at and lovelier to eat.
When whipping cream, beat only until stiff peaks form.*

8 eggs, separated

2 cups plus 2 tablespoons sugar

1 cup lemon juice

1 teaspoon grated lemon

2 1/2 cups heavy cream

Strawberries (garnish)

1. Preheat oven to 225°.

2. Whisk egg whites until stiff, then gradually beat in 1 1/2 cups sugar. Beat again until the meringue is smooth and glossy. Pour the meringue into 1 12-inch or 2 9-inch round baking dishes. Bake for 1 1/2 hours, or until the meringue has dried out but is still pale in color. When meringue has been allowed to cool, form a well in the center by pressing down the cooked meringue with the back of a spoon, leaving a border about 1-inch wide.

3. In the top of a double boiler, heat the egg yolks and 1/2 cup of sugar. Using a wire whisk, stir in the lemon juice and lemon rind. Cook for about 12 minutes, or until the custard has thickened, whisking constantly.

4. Beat 2 cups of cream until stiff and fold into the custard. Pour into the meringue nest and chill for 24 hours.

5. Just before serving, beat the remaining cream and 2 tablespoons of sugar and spread over the lemon custard. Garnish with strawberries.

Crustless Ricotta Pie

From Pennsport **Italian** ***Serves 8-10***

For best results, drain the ricotta through a sieve. This will reduce any weeping during cooking.

3 pounds ricotta	1 teaspoon ground cinnamon
1 dozen eggs	1 teaspoon vanilla extract
1 cup sugar	1/2 pint heavy cream

1. Preheat oven to 350°.

2. In a large mixing bowl, food processor or blender, mix all ingredients thoroughly for about 5 minutes. When smooth, pour into a 9-inch baking dish.

3. Place baking dish into a large pan filled halfway up with water. Bake for 1-1 1/2 hours, or until a knife inserted comes out clean.

4. Cool and refrigerate overnight.

Variation: Add lemon zest to the mixture or sprinkle zest on top of the pie.

Tropical Fruit Salad with Grand Marnier and Ginger Syrup

From Fairmount   *Serves 4*

This is a very light and refreshing dessert, but with a kind of sophistication that would end any meal on an elegant note.

2 ripe kiwis

1 cup fresh strawberries

1 cup blueberries

1 whole pineapple, peeled and sliced

Peaches, peeled and sliced

GRAND MARNIER AND GINGER SYRUP

2 cups water

1/2 cup sugar

1-inch piece of ginger root, cut into thin strips

1/4 cup Grand Marnier

1. Prepare the Grand Marnier and ginger syrup. In a saucepan, mix the water, sugar and ginger strips together. Bring to a boil and cook for about 10 minutes. Cool and add the Grand Marnier.

2. Arrange the prepared fruits attractively on a large platter or on individual plates. Pour on the Grand Marnier and ginger syrup. Chill and serve.

Noodle Pudding

From Washington Square **Jewish** *Serves 10*

This recipe has many variations, but the apricots add a lovely taste, and using cream cheese gives this pudding a creamier flavor.

1 1/2 pounds medium egg noodles

12 eggs

1 8-ounce package cream cheese, at room temperature

1/2 pound (2 sticks) butter or margarine, at room temperature

1/2 cup sugar, or to taste

1/2 cup milk

1 tablespoon lemon juice

2 cups canned apricots, drained

Graham cracker crumbs

1. Boil the noodles for 15 minutes and drain.

2. Preheat oven to 350°.

3. Butter the bottom of a large baking pan or lasagna pan.

4. In a bowl, blender or food processor, mix the eggs, cream cheese, margarine, sugar, milk and lemon juice until smooth. Pour into the noodles and blend well.

5. Pour half the noodle mixture into the buttered pan and spread on the chopped apricots. Top with the remaining noodle mixture. Sprinkle graham cracker crumbs over the noodles and bake for 1 1/4 to 1 1/2 hours. Cool and cut into squares.

Serving suggestion: Noodle pudding can be served with a dollop of sour cream and/or cherries.

Nalesniki
Cheese-Filled Crepes

From Queen Village　　**Polish**　　*Makes about 12 crepes*

These crepes are simple to make and can be made ahead and filled when needed. The choices for fillings are endless. In addition to the cheese, try apple butter, jams or preserves.

BATTER
1 cup flour

2 cups milk, at room temperature

1 egg

1/2 teaspoon vanilla extract

Pinch of salt

Butter or shortening for cooking crepes

CHEESE FILLING
1 1/2 pounds farmer's or pot cheese (dry cottage cheese)

1 egg

3 tablespoons sugar

1/2 teaspoon cinnamon

1/2 teaspoon salt

1. Mix all batter ingredients together with beater or mixer. Batter should be smooth with the consistency of gravy. If batter is too thin, add flour; if too thick, add milk.

2. In an 8 1/2-inch skillet (or a 6-inch skillet for smaller crepes), add a little butter or shortening to grease bottom of pan. Heat until hot. With a ladle, pour about 2 ounces of batter into skillet. Rotate pan until entire surface is covered. Work quickly. When edges are dry, turn crepe and cook other side. Regrease pan each time.

3. Prepare cheese filling by mixing together all ingredients. Spread evenly on each crepe and roll.

Serving suggestion: For a special summer treat, top with sliced and sweetened fresh strawberries.

Cheese Blintzes

From the Northeast   **Jewish**   *Makes 10 blintzes*

BATTER
3 eggs
4 tablespoons flour
1/2 cup water
Pinch of salt
Vegetable shortening for frying blintzes
1 cup sour cream for topping blintzes

CHEESE FILLING
1 pound farmer's or pot cheese (dry cottage cheese)
1 ounce cream cheese, at room temperature
1 heaping tablespoon sugar
Dash of ground cinnamon

1. Mix together the eggs, flour, water and salt to make a thin batter.

2. In a 6-inch skillet, add a little vegetable shortening to form a thin film in pan. Place over medium-high heat until hot. Pour in 3 tablespoons of batter and immediately turn and tilt the pan so that batter covers the surface evenly and makes a very thin pancake. Fry until lightly brown on underside. Top will start to bubble and set.

3. To make cheese filling, combine all ingredients in a bowl. Place about 2 tablespoons of filling down the center of each pancake and roll the sides over the filling to close. Fry until lightly brown on both sides. Repeat with remaining batter, regreasing pan before making each pancake. Already-filled blintzes can be kept in a warm oven while preparing others.

4. Serve with a generous dollop of sour cream.

Old-Fashioned Rice Pudding

From Roxborough   *Serves 6 1-cup portions.*

This version of an old-time favorite has a light, delicate, creamy texture.

1 cup long-grain rice   3/4 cup sugar
5 1/2 cups milk   Cinnamon
3 1/2 cups light cream

1. In a large saucepan, pour in milk and cream and heat to a boil.

2. Stir in rice, reduce heat to low and cook for 30 minutes, making sure to stir mixture occasionally during cooking process to prevent sticking and scorching.

3. Add the sugar, stir and cook another 45 minutes or until creamy. Continue to stir occasionally during cooking. Stir constantly for the last 10 minutes of cooking time. Most of the liquid, but not all, will be evaporated. During cooking the mixture should be bubbling lightly, but not at a roaring boil.

4. Remove pudding from heat and pour into 6 individual dessert cups or 1 large bowl. Sprinkle with cinnamon and allow to cool. Refrigerate when cool.

Breads

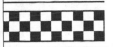

Mondel Bread

From Fairmount   **Jewish**   *Makes 5 dozen slices*

This bread is excellent served at breakfast or tea time.

4 eggs
1 1/2 cups sugar
1 cup oil
4 cups flour
2 1/2 teaspoons baking powder
1 teaspoon salt
2 teaspoons ground cinnamon

3 teaspoons vanilla extract
2 teaspoons almond extract
3/4 cup raisins, plumped in 1/4
  cup boiling water

CINNAMON SUGAR
1/4 cup sugar mixed with 1
  teaspoon ground cinnamon

1. Preheat oven to 350°.

2. Beat eggs, sugar and oil together. Beat in flour, baking powder, salt, cinnamon and extracts. Stir in raisins with liquid.
Batter will be very thick, like cookie dough.

3. Lightly grease a jelly-roll pan or cookie sheet 10 x 15 inches
and spread dough out evenly. Bake for about 20 minutes,
or until firm to touch. When done, slice lengthwise in thirds,
and then into 1/2-inch strips. Turn slices on side and sprinkle with cinnamon sugar. Bake 10 minutes, then turn again
and bake another 10-15 minutes.

Taralli Twists
Pepper Ring Bread

From South Philadelphia   **Italian**   *Makes 25-30 3-inch rings*

This braided bread is wonderful for parties or for snacking. Using whole black peppercorns, freshly ground, makes quite a difference to the peppery flavor of this bread.

1 package dry yeast (preferably cake yeast, if available)

3 cups water

2 pounds flour

1/4 cup olive oil

1 tablespoon coarsely ground black pepper

2 tablespoons salt

1. In 1 cup lukewarm water, dissolve the yeast. Add this to the flour, oil, black pepper, salt and remaining 2 cups of water. Knead mixture for approximately 10 minutes, or until dough is smooth (with the consistency of pasta dough). While kneading, flour hands to prevent stickiness.

2. Roll the dough into the shape of a loaf of French bread and allow to rest for 15 minutes.

3. Cut dough into slices. Roll the slices into ropes, then braid. Connect the two ends together to form a circle about 3-4 inches in diameter. (Taralli twists resemble bagels that have been braided.)

4. Plunge the twists into a pot of boiling water, 4 at a time. They should rise to the surface in a minute or so. If they do not, remove them from the water anyway. Allow them to dry on a dishcloth for 10 minutes.

5. Preheat oven to 400°.

6. On a baking sheet, cook the twists for 35-40 minutes, or to the desired degree of brownness. They can be frozen and reheated.

Pumpkin Bread

From Center City   *Makes 4 1-pound loaves*

This is another moist, sweet bread. The topping adds a wonderful glaze and goes well with the pumpkin.

1 cup (2 sticks) butter

3 cups sugar

4 eggs

2/3 cup water

3 1/3 cups flour

1 teaspoon vanilla extract

1 teaspoon ground cinnamon

1 teaspoon ground nutmeg

1 1/2 teaspoons salt

2 cups canned pumpkin

2 teaspoons baking soda

1 cup chopped walnuts

TOPPING

6 tablespoons brown sugar

3 tablespoons butter

3 tablespoons milk

1. Preheat oven to 350°.

2. Cream butter and sugar together. Add in all remaining ingredients and mix well.

3. Pour batter into 4 1-pound loaf pans and bake for approximately 1 hour.

4. Make topping. In a saucepan, combine ingredients and bring to a boil. Spread over warm pumpkin bread.

Irish Soda Bread

From Schuylkill   **Irish**   ***Makes 1 round loaf***

Soda bread is one of the specialties of Ireland and is very easy to make. The apple cider vinegar in this recipe adds moistness to the bread.

2 1/2 cups flour	1/2 cup butter or margarine
1 teaspoon baking soda	1/2 cup seedless raisins
1 teaspoon baking powder	2 teaspoons caraway seeds
1/2 teaspoon salt	3 tablespoons apple cider
2 tablespoons sugar	vinegar
	3/4 cup milk

1. Preheat oven to 400°.

2. Sift together the dry ingredients. Cut in the butter and mix until it resembles fine cornmeal. (A food processor can be used to mix the ingredients, but stir in the raisins and caraway seeds.)

3. Add the raisins and caraway seeds.

4. Make a well in the center of the dry mixture, add the apple cider vinegar and milk, then stir vigorously with a fork until the mixture is moistened.

5. Turn onto a lightly floured board and knead gently 8-10 times, then shape into a round ball and place on a greased 8-inch pie dish. Make 1 or 2 slashes across the top and brush with a little milk. Bake for 15 minutes, then lower heat to 375° and cook for a further 30 minutes, or until a toothpick comes out clean. Remove to a wire rack to cool. Cut into wedges and serve.

Serving suggestion: Excellent served warm and spread with butter.

Cornmeal Cracklin Bread

From Germantown **Soul Food** *Serves 6*

Cracklin, which is fried pork rind, is slightly chewy but adds good flavor to the cornbread.

2 cups white cornmeal
1 teaspoon salt
3 teaspoons baking powder
1/2 cup cold water

1/2 cup milk
1 egg, beaten
1/2 cup cracklin, chopped into
    large pea-size pieces

1. Preheat oven to 400°.

2. Sift together cornmeal, salt and baking powder.

3. Stir in water, milk and egg. Beat until smooth.

4. Stir in cracklin. Pour into a greased 9-inch skillet and bake for 30-35 minutes. Cut into wedges and serve hot.

Zucchini Bread

From Northern Liberties   *Makes 2 loaves*

A very delicious version of zucchini bread.

3 eggs, lightly beaten

1 cup vegetable oil

2 cups sugar

3 cups zucchini, grated and well
   drained

3 teaspoons vanilla extract

3 cups flour

1 teaspoon salt

3 teaspoons ground cinnamon

2 teaspoons baking powder

3 teaspoons baking soda

1 cup walnuts, chopped

1 cup raisins

1. Preheat oven to 350°.

2. In a large bowl, mix together eggs, oil, sugar, zucchini and vanilla extract.

3. Add flour, salt, cinnamon, baking powder and baking soda. Mix thoroughly. Stir in walnuts and raisins. (The walnuts and raisins may be omitted, but they add a nice texture to the bread.)

4. Grease 2 bread pans (9 x 5 x 3 inches) and pour mixture evenly into both. Bake in oven for 1 hour. Cool slightly in pan, then remove and cool on a rack.

Chappati
Flat Bread

From West Philadelphia   **Indian**   *Makes about*
15 rounds

Chappati is unleavened and is probably one of the most popular
Indian breads. It is very easy to make.

1 pound whole-wheat flour
1 teaspoon salt
1 cup lukewarm water

1. Place the flour and salt in a large bowl. Slowly add the
water, mixing until it forms a soft dough. Knead the dough
by hand, in a food processor or mixer, for a few minutes,
or until smooth. Cover with a damp cloth and leave to rest
for 1/2 hour.

2. Heat a skillet (preferably cast-iron) until very hot.

3. Meanwhile, knead the dough briefly again and divide into
about 15 pieces. The dough will be a little sticky. Flour your
hands, take one piece of dough, form a ball and then press
into a round disk about 5 1/2 inches in diameter.

4. Shake off excess flour and place chappati into the hot pan.
Let the dough cook for about 1 minute; white spots should
form underneath. Turn over and cook another 1/2 minute
on the other side. The chappati should be slightly puffed.
To reheat, wrap in foil and bake for 20-30 minutes at 425°.

Serving suggestion: Serve with any curry dish or a vegetable
curry (page 184).

Index